The Philosophy and Life of Mulla Sadra

The Philosophy and Life of Mulla Sadra

2013

London Academy of Iranian Studies

Seyed G Safavi

Copyright © 2013 by Seyed G Safavi.

Library of Congress Control Number: 2013914760
ISBN: Softcover 978-1-4836-8483-3

All rights reserved. No part of this book may be reproduced or transmitted in any form or by any means, electronic or mechanical, including photocopying, recording, or by any information storage and retrieval system, without permission in writing from the copyright owner.

This book was printed in the United States of America.

Rev. date: 09/17/2013

To order additional copies of this book, contact:
Xlibris LLC
1-888-795-4274
www.Xlibris.com
Orders@Xlibris.com
46875

Contents

Introduction 7
Chapter 1: Mulla Sadra's Life, A Short Biography 11
Chapter 2: Mulla Sadra's Transcendent Philosophy 30
Chapter 3: God in Greek and Islamic Philosophy: A Comparative Study of Aristotle and Mulla Sadra Shirazi on the Necessary Existent 83
Chapter 4: Rumi and Mulla Sadra on Theoretical and Practical Intellect 115
Chapter 5: Mulla Sadra and Descartes On the Soul: A Philosophical Comparison 124
Index 139

INTRODUCTION

Mulla Sadra, known also as Sadr al-Muta'allihin, was born in Shiraz, Iran, in the year 1571-1572 AD and died in 1640 AD. His writings focus on philosophy and commentaries on the Qur'an and *Al-Usul Al-Kafi*. His most important philosophical writings include *Al-Asfar Al-Arba'at Al-'Aqliyyah*, *Al-Shawahid Al-Rububiyya*, *Al-Hikamat Al-'Arshiyya*, *Kitab Al-Masha'ir*, and *Al-Mabda' wa Al-Ma'ad*.

The present work consists of five chapters, written on two categories: The Transcendent Philosophy and Mulla Sadra's School, and Comparative Studies of Mulla Sadra and Other Philosophers. Several years of work has enabled me to complete some parts of this project, which concerns the relation of Mulla Sadra to the totality of the Islamic tradition, and the characteristics of his 'Transcendent Philosophy' being used in its original sense.

Chapter One of this book discusses Mulla Sadra's life, one of the greatest Muslim Iranian philosopher and founding father of the 'Transcendent Philosophy'.

Chapter Two discusses Mulla Sadra's philosophy, entitled 'Transcendent philosophy', in 3 sections:, the definition of 'Transcendent philosophy', the 16 principles of Mulla Sadra's philosophy, and Mulla Sadra's views on different schools of thought, such as Ancient Metaphysicians, Greek and Muslim philosophers. This is an original work in the English language as it presents the most important aspects of Mulla Sadra's philosophy based directly on his various writings in Arabic language, such as *Asfar*, *al-Shawahid al-rububiyya*, *al-Mabda' wa l-Ma'ad*, *Arshiyyah*, *al-Masha'ir* and *Mafatih al-Ghayb*.

Chapter Three is entitled 'A Comparative Study of Aristotle and Mulla Sadra Shirazi on the Necessary Existent'. The nature of God, or the demiurge-creator and designer of the cosmos, is a venerable subject in philosophy and natural theology. In the Abrahamic faiths, and especially within a philosophical context, most medieval religious discussion about God, including the ontological and cosmological proofs for His existence, stems from the famous proof of the Prime Unmoved Mover in Aristotle's *Physics*. It was this proof, alongside later, more ontological proofs, associated with Anselm and Avicenna, that underpinned medieval philosophical theology. For this reason it is instructive to trace the development of philosophical theology from Aristotle through to the more sophisticated arguments about God found in the later Islamic tradition. In tracing this development we can see the creative thought of the monotheists who discuss God within a broadly Aristotelian context, and with reference to Aristotelian axioms. The present chapter begins with Aristotle's theology—his concept of God and His attributes—and then compares this architectonic, foundational theology to the later theology of Mulla Sadra, which represents a richer and more sophisticated concept of God, indicative of a mature and confident Islamic philosophical tradition.

Chapter Four discusses Rumi and Mulla Sadra on Theoretical and Practical Intellect.

Rumi (1207-1273) the great Persian sage identified approximately 34 different varieties of intellect in his masterpiece Mathnawi. They may be categorised into three main types:

1- Meta-theoretical and Practical intellect, also known as Universal Intellect and First Intellect.
2- Theoretical intellect, used to perceive and distinguish between truth and untruth. According to Rumi, theoretical intellect corresponds with faithful intellect, perfect intellect, honourable intellect and Divine seeing intellect.
3- Practical intellect, which serves to distinguish between Good and Evil. Rumi held that practical intellect included material reason, resurrection intellect, partial reason, popular reason, and brief reason.

According to Rumi everyone has intellect, and in a perfect man, intellect may help him transcend Particular Reason to arrive at Universal intellect.

According to the great Iranian Muslim philosopher Mulla Sadra (979-1571), there are four types of Theoretical and Practical intellect, all of which are based on perfection. Theoretical intellect ascends from "material intellect" (*'aql hayuluni*), "habitual intellect" (*'aql bi al-malakeh*), "intellect in act" (*'aql bi al-fi'l*) to the "acquired intellect" (*'aql bi al mustafad*).

Practical intellect may be divided into the following processes: polishing/refinement of the apparent/outer part, polishing the inner part, illuminating the heart, and annihilation of the soul from its essence.

According to Mulla Sadra's transcendent philosophy, which is based on "principality of Being" (*asalat wujud*), each act of knowing involves the being of the knower, and the hierarchy of the faculties of knowledge correspond to the hierarchy of existence. Reason is in its essence a Divine light.

Chapter Five, entitled 'Mulla Sadra and Descartes On the Soul: A Philosophical Comparison', examines the philosophical views of Mulla Sadra and Descartes on the soul. The comparison is divided into five main segments, as follows:

1. An Exposition of Mulla Sadra's Discussion of the Soul
2. An Exposition of Descartes' Discussion of the Soul
3. Similarities and Differences Between the Two
4. Strengths of Mulla Sadra's Theory
5. Critiques of Descartes' Theory

The foundation of Mulla Sadra's theory is "the corporeality of contingency and the spirituality of subsistence in relation to the soul." The foundation of Descartes' theory is "the real distinction between the substance of the soul and the body." Mulla Sadra's theory includes a philosophical proof for physical resurrection, whereas Descartes' dualism led to the collapse of his philosophical system.

This book is one of the best books in the English language on Mulla Sadra's philosophy and is useful for university students in the field of Islamic studies and Islamic philosophy.

Seyed G Safavi
London Academy of Iranian Studies
August 7, 2013

Mulla Sadra's Life, A Short Biography

From Shiraz to Najaf, In Search of The Truth:

Sadreddin Muhammad ibn Ibrahim Qawami Shirazi, commonly known as Mulla Sadra, and also as Sadr al-Muta'alehin, was born in Shiraz in southern Iran in 979 A.H., 1571-1572 C.E., and died in 1050 A.H., 1640 C.E in Basra.[1] He is buried in the shrine of Imam Ali ('a) in Najaf.

He spent his youth in Shiraz where he studied some of the introductory Islamic sciences. Thereafter he moved to Isfahan to further pursue his Islamic studies. While in Isfahan he studied the intellectual and narrative sciences of Islam under two of the greatest Islamic scholars: namely, Sheikh Baha' al-Din al-'Amili (d.1031/1622) and Seyyed Muhammad Baqir Astarabadi, also known as Mir Damad (d.1040/1631).

Due to his hard work, the high degree of his intelligence, his spiritual capacity, and the purity of his heart, Mulla Sadra became a master of the field of metaphysics, providing commentary on the Quran and the sciences of hadith. Due to Mulla Sadra's exalted spiritual status, his deep understanding of the esoteric dimensions of Islam, and his promotion of this knowledge in a simple language understandable by the masses (in contrast to the complicated language of Mir Damad) he became a target of abuse by ignorant scholars of the exoteric sciences, in reference to whom Rumi says:

"He knows a hundred thousand superfluous matters connected with the (various) sciences,(but) that unjust man does not know his own soul.

He knows the special properties of every substance, (but) in elucidating his own substance (essence) he is (as ignorant) as an ass.

Saying "I know (what is) permissible and impermissible," thou knowest not whether thou thyself are permissible or (impermissible as) an old woman.

Thou knowest this licit (thing) and that illicit (thing), but art thou licit or illicit? Consider well!

Thou knowest what is the value of every merchandise; (if) thou knowest not the value of thyself, 'tis folly.

Thou has become acquainted with the fortunate and inauspicious stars; thou does not look to see whether thou art fortunate or unwashed (spiritually foul and ill-favored)

This, this, is the soul of all the sciences: that thou should know who thou shalt be on the Day of Judgment."[2]

The abuse of the scholars of the exoteric sciences forced him to realize that he needed to go into *Khalwa*t (isolation) in order to reach union with the Universal Intellect, so that his intellect may become Divine. There, the veils of the material world would be removed for him, helping him achieve the Divine intuitive knowledge he sought, as Imam Sadiq notes. So he isolated himself from society and spent his time sincerely worshipping his exalted Lord in Kahak a small village near Qum, where he spent some seven years-eleven years.

As Mulla Sadra says:

"Indeed we spent our life in search of knowledge;

However, the search did not earn us much but grievances.

Our entire life was wasted in matters related to other than the Beloved;

Excepting regret, we had no share therein

O cup-bearer circulate among us the cup [of Divine gnosis]

So that the time I lost is covered up."[3]

He continues:

"Therefore when I found that the place was bereft of one who acknowledged the sanctity of the secrets and the sciences of the pure-hearted, and that gnosis and its mysteries have vanished and the truth and its light has been effaced . . . I abandoned the people of my time and concealed myself from them. Thus the tranquility of my perspicacity and the stillness of nature came to my rescue from the enmity of the age and the impotence of my rambles, until I isolated myself in a place by the outskirts of the city and in a state of apathy and dejection hid myself; this happened while I experienced despair and broken-heartedness and while I engaged in compulsory acts of worship and struggled to cover up the excesses I had committed in the presence of Allah. In that particular state I neither taught nor engaged in writing; for writing on matters of gnosis, refuting the incorrect ideas, elucidating the objectives and removing the difficulties are among those things that require the lavation of one's intellect and purification of one's faculty of imagination from those things that result in restlessness and confusion . . . Thus I turned instinctively towards the Source of all the means, and naturally expressed my humbleness in front of the Simplifier of the difficulties; and when I remained in this particular state of concealment and isolation and obscurity and seclusion for a long time, my soul was enlightened through spiritual struggle and my heart was powerfully lit up through many austerities (*riyazat*). This made the celestial rays of light pour down into my spirit; and the mysteries of the realm of Divine Omnipotence (*jabarut*) were untangled for me; and the rays of unity touched my spirit and the Divine grace embraced it. Hence I came to learn of secrets I had not yet known, and mysteries that had not been clear through intellectual proof were now unraveled for me. I witnessed more details by way of vision and spiritual disclosure than I had known before through intellectual proof . . ."[4]

"And it is highly probable that this distinction, that this blessed servant, who hails from the blessed Islamic community, attained through the great Bestower, Who is Generous and Merciful, was only due to his frequent occupation in acquiring this lofty aim and his extreme perseverance in front of the ignorant and degenerate folk, and [because of] the inadequate concern of the people for him, and the absence of mutual understanding with him; to such an extent that he lived in the world in a state of grief and sorrow and neither occupied the lowest position from the seminarians in front of the people, nor in front of their scholars, most of whom were more wretched than the ignorant masses themselves; and this was due to the fact that apart from prattling they knew no other path of acquiring knowledge; and because of their limited outlook on human perfection and development, which they thought could not be achieved save through the discussion of vanities.

When the Eternal Divine Mercy encompassed me, the radiations of Divine unity and the grace of the Self-subsistent Sovereignty (*al-Altaf al-Qayyumiyyah*) touched me, my soul experienced spiritual repose from their admissions and refutations and was freed from their inflictions and whisperings. Then Allah taught me the secrets and mysteries that I had not known and the realities pertaining to lordship and Divine gnosis were unraveled for me; realities that had not been thus unraveled by means of intellectual proof."[5]

"And it is forbidden as a divine decree and impossible by Divine predestination that the knowledge of these four disciplines are comprehended, especially the gnosis of the Essence and the Hereafter, save by relinquishing the present world and seeking seclusion and abstaining from worldly fame; besides possessing a brilliant perspicacity, a critical bent of mind, extreme intelligence, a pure disposition and a very quick intellectual power of analysis."[6]

"And verily I know—praise be to Allah—through visual certainty that this narrative and its like that have appeared in the Book of God and the narratives of the immaculate souls concerning the states of Resurrection and its horrors are true and correct. Therefore I have believed in it by witnessing, and by association with, intuitive knowledge and Divine vision . . ."[7]

In the year 1040 A.H., Mulla Sadra returned to Shiraz, where he taught until the last years of his life.

Mulla Sadra, in his introduction to the commentary of *Ayat al-Kursi*, clearly introduces himself as *"an inhabitant of Qum."* In that text he also says, *"Verily [I am] more than forty years of age"*; and, taking into consideration his date of birth, that would have been in approximately the year 1022 A.H. Thus, most probably he lived in Qum between the years of 1023 A.H. and 1040 A.H. However, the introduction of his *Asfar* indicates that he lived in Qum for years before his writings:

He says:

"Until the time I secluded myself in an area by the outskirts of the city, in a state of apathy and dejection I hid myself; this happened while I experienced despair and broken-heartedness and while I engaged in compulsory acts of worship and strove to cover up the excesses I had committed in the Presence of Allah. In that particular state I neither taught nor engaged in writing."[8]

There is not much information concerning his family, but we know that he had a distinguished son, Mirza Ibrahim, who was a scholar of Islamic sciences. His grandson also named Muhammad Ibn Ibrahim was an eminent scholar as well.

His Tutors:

Mulla Sadra's main masters were Mir Damad and Sheikh Bahia. Mir Mohammad Baqer Asterabadi (d. 1631 or 1632), known also as Mir Damad, was an Iranian philosopher in the Islamic Peripatetic Neoplatonizing tradition of Ibn Sina. He was also the central founder of the School of Isfahan, which embraced a theosophical outlook known as *hikmat-i ilahi* (divine wisdom). He was known by his students and admirers as the Third Teacher (*mu'alim al-thalith*) after Aristotle and Farabi.

His major contribution to Islamic philosophy was his formulation of the gradations of time, and the emanations of the separate categories of time, as divine hypostases. He resolved the controversy of the createdness or uncreatedness of the world in time by proposing the notion of *huduth-e-dahri* (atemporal origination), an explanation that was grounded in, and yet transcended, Avicennian and Suhrawardian categories. In brief, he argued that with the exception of God, all things, including the earth and the heavenly bodies, have both eternal and temporal origins. He influenced the revival of *al-falsafa al-yamani* (Philosophy of Yemen), a philosophy based on revelation and the sayings of the prophets, rather than on the rationalism of the Greeks.

Mir Damad's many treatises on Islamic philosophy include *Taqwim al-Iman* (Calendars of Faith*)*, a treasured account of creation and divine knowledge, the *Kitab Qabasat al-Ilahiyah* (Book of the Divine Embers of Fiery Kindling), wherein he lays out his concept of atemporal origination, *Kitab al-Jadhawat* (Book of Spiritual Attractions) and *Sirat al-Mustaqim* (The Straight Path). He wrote poetry under the pseudonym *Ishraq* (Illumination); he also wrote books on mathematics, although these are of secondary importance.

Bahā' al-Dīn Muḥammad ibn Ḥusayn al-'Āmilī (1547-1621), known also as Shaykh-i Bahā'ī, was' a philosopher, architect, mathematician, astronomer and poet. He was one of the main founders of the Isfahan School of Islamic Philosophy. He was also a mystic. He had a distinct Sufi leaning for which he was criticized by Mohammad Baqer Majlesi. During his travels he dressed like a Dervish and frequented Sufi circles. He also appeared in the circles of both the Nurbakhshi and the Ni'matullāhī Sufi orders. In the work *Resāla fi'l-waḥda al-wojūdīya* (Exposition of the concept of *Wahdat al-Wujud* or Unity of Existences), he states that the Sufis are the true believers, calls for an unbiased assessment of their utterances, and refers to his own mystical experiences. His Persian poetry is also replete with mystical allusions and symbols. That said, Shaykh Baha' al-Din's texts call for strict adherence to the *Sharia* as a prerequisite for embarking on the *Tariqah*; he did not hold a high opinion view of antinomian mysticism. Shaykh Baha' al-Din contributed numerous works of philosophy, logic, astronomy and mathematics, including 88 articles, epistles and books. His outstanding works in the Iranian language are *Jame' Abbasi* and two *masnavis* known as *Shir wa Shikar* (Milk and Sugar) and *Nan wa Halwa* (Bread and Halva). His other work *Kashkool* includes stories, discussions of scientific topics, and Persian and Arabic proverbs. He wrote *Khulasat Al-Hisab* and *Tashrih Al-Aflak* in Arabic.

His Students:

Among his most popular students were his sons-in-law, Mulla Mohsen Fayz Kashani and Mulla 'Abd al-Razzaq Lahiji, whom he nicknamed Fayz and Fayyaz, respectively.

Of the two, Fayz was more inspired by Mulla Sadra. Fayz was also among the great narrators of tradition and was well-acquainted with the narrative sciences.

Fayyaz, known also as Mulla 'Abd al-Razzaq bin Husayn Lahiji, was a scholar, philosopher, theologian and poet, and the author of *al-Shawariq*. He lived and studied in Qum, where he benefited from Mulla Sadra's teachings, and was among his great students. Fayyaz is known to have been more penetrating in his analysis of issues than Fayz (however, Fayz's knowledge of the different sciences was wider). Fayyaz opposed Mulla Sadra on some of his philosophical principles, the most popular of which was the principality of existence.

Another of Mulla Sadra's notable students was Shaykh Husayn Tankabuni. A treatise which he wrote on the temporal createdness of the world was printed in the margins of Mulla Sadra's *al-Mashahir*.

Mulla Sadra's writings:

His Writings in Chronological Order:

Mulla Sadra's philosophy matured gradually over his lifetime. He reached his zenith of perfection during the final years of his life. A look at his writings in chronological order is of the utmost importance. We must also remember that he was engaged in writing his magnum opus *al-Asfar al-Arba'ah* throughout his blessed life.

Here is the list of his works, both those that have been definitively attributed to him, and those speculated to be his:

1. *Al-Mabda' wa'l Ma'ad*
2. *Sharh al-Hidayah*
3. *Tafsir Surah al-Hadid*
4. *Tafsir Surah al-'A'la*
5. *Tafsir Ayah al-Kursi*, after 1020 AH.
6. *Tafsir Ayah al-Nur*, after 1030 AH.
7. *Tafsir Surah al-Tariq*, after 1030 AH.
8. *Tafsir Surah al-sajdah*
9. *Tafsir Surah Yasin*, after 1030 AH.
10. *Tafsir Surah al-Waqi'ah*
11. *Al-Shawahid al-Rububiyyah*
12. *Tafsir Surah al-Zilzal*
13. *Risalah al-huduth*
14. *Ta'liqat Hikmah al-Ishriq*, after 1041 AH.
15. *Kasr Asnam al-Jahiliyyah*
16. *Tafsir Surah al-Jumu'ah*
17. *Mafitih al-Ghaib*
18. *Tafsir Surah al-Hamd*
19. *Tafsir Surah al-Baqarah*
20. *Mutashabihat al-Quran*
21. *Asrar al-Ayat*
22. *Al-Hikmah al-'arshiyyah*
23. *Ta'liqat al-Shifa'*
24. *Ajwibah al-masail al-nasiriyyah*
25. *Sharh al-Usul min al-Kafi*, 1044 AH.

Mulla Sadra's Works:

His well-known books that have been published so far include the following:

"1. *Al-Hikmat al-muta'aliyah fi'l-asfar al-arba'ah*

The discussions in this book begin with the issues of being and quiddity, and continue with the issues of motion, time, perception, substance, and accident. One part is devoted to proving the existence of God and His attributes; this book ends with a discussion of man's soul, and the subjects of death and resurrection. Interestingly, the themes considered in this interesting and important book are organized according to the four stages of gnostic spiritual and mystic journeys, with each stage considered as one journey. Thus the book begins with Existence and continues with the Hereafter, God, and the mustered people; this reflects the first stage of a gnostic's journey, in which he travels from himself and his people towards God. In the second and third stages the gnostic moves from God to God (from His Essence to His Attributes and Acts), and, in the fourth stage, the Gnostic moves from God to people. The original book is in four large volumes, which have been published in nine small volumes, several times.

In fact, this book is a philosophical encyclopaedia, a collection of important issues discussed in Islamic philosophy, enriched by the ideas of earlier philosophers, from Pythagoras to Mulla Sadra's contemporaries. It contains responses based on strong new arguments. All of these features have made it the book of choice for teaching higher levels of philosophical education in scientific and religious centers.

The composition of the book began around 1015 AH (1605 AD); it was completed sometime after 1040 AH (1630 AD).

2. *Al-Tafsir* (Commentary on the Qur'an)

During his life, Mulla Sadra interpreted some of the chapters (*Surahs*) of the Qur'an. In the last decade of his life, he began to compile all his interpretations into a complete work (beginning with the early chapters of the Holy Book), but death did not allow him to finish this task. The names of the chapters he interpreted, in approximate chronological order, are as follows:

1. Chapter *al-Hadid*, 2. *Commentary on Ayat al-kursi* 3. Chapter *Sajdah*, 4. Chapter *al-Zilzal*, 5. Verses *al-Nur, al-Yasin, al-Tariq*, 6. Chapter *al-A'la*, 7.

Chapter: *al-Waqi'ah*, 8. Chapter: *al-Fatihah*, 9. Chapter: *al-Jumu'ah*, and 10. Chapter: *al-Baqarah*.

In bibliographies of Mulla Sadra's works, each of the above appears independently, but we have cited them all under the title, *Commentary on the Qur'an*. Mulla Sadra also wrote two other books on the Qur'an, called *Mafatih al-qayb* and *Asrar al-ayat*, which are considered introductions to the interpretation of the Qur'an, and represent the philosophy behind this task.

3. *Sharh al-hidayah*

This work is a commentary on a book called *Hidayah*, which was written on the basis of Peripatetic philosophy, and was previously used to provide students with a preliminary introduction to philosophy. However, it is rarely used today.

4. *Al-Mabda' wa'l-ma'ad*

Also called *al-Hikmat al-muta'aliyyah*, this book is a summary of the second half of *Asfar*. It does not include any of the discussions that Mulla Sadra viewed as useless and unnecessary. He called this book *The Beginning and the End* due to his belief that philosophy means knowledge of the Origin, and knowledge of the Return. This book is mainly dedicated to issues related to theology and eschatology, and is considered one of Mulla Sadra's most important books.

5. *al-Mazahir*

This book is similar to *al-Mabda' wa'l-ma'ad*, but is shorter. It is, in fact, a handbook designed to familiarize readers with Mulla Sadra's philosophy.

6. *Huduth al-'alam*

For many philosophers, the origin of the world is a complicated and debatable problem. In this book, in addition to quoting the theories of pre—and post-Socratic philosophers, and those of some Muslim philosophers, Mulla Sadra proves his account of the origin of the world, using the theory of trans-substantial motion.

7. *Iksir al-'arifin*

As the name suggests, this is a gnostic and educational book.

8. *Al-Hashr*

The central theme of this book is the quality of existents' resurrection in the Hereafter. Here, Mulla Sadra expresses the theory of the resurrection of objects and animals in the Hereafter.

9. *Al-Masha'ir*

This is a short but rich and profound book on existence and related subjects. Professor Henry Corbin has translated it into French, and written an introduction to it. It has also been recently translated into English.

10. *Al-Waridat al-qalbiyyah*

In this book, Mulla Sadra presents a brief account of important philosophical problems. It seems to be an inventory of the Divine inspirations and illuminations he had received throughout his life.

11. *Iqad al-na'imin*

This book is about theoretical and actual gnosis, and the science of monotheism. It presents some guidelines and instructional points to wake the sleeping.

12. *Al-Masa'il al-qudsiyyah*

This booklet deals mainly with issues such as existence in mind and epistemology. Here, Mulla Sadra combines epistemology and ontology.

13. *'Arshiyyah*

Also called *al-Hikmat al-'arshiyyah*, this is another guide to Mull Sadra's philosophy. As in *al-Mazahir*, he tries to demonstrate *he* Beginning and the End concisely but precisely. Professor James Winston Maurice has translated this book into English, and has written an informative introduction to it.

14. *Al-Shawadhid al-rububiyyah*

This philosophical book is mainly written in the Illuminationist style, and represents Mulla Sadra's ideas during the early period of his philosophical thoughts.

15. *Sharh-i shifa*

Mulla Sadra wrote this book as a commentary upon some of the issues discussed in the section on theology (*Ilahiyyat*) in Ibn Sina's *al-Shifa*. *Sharh-i shifa* has also been published in the form of glosses clearly expressing Mulla Sadra's ideas on this topic.

16. *Sharh-i hikmat al-ishraq*

This work is a useful and profound commentary, or collection of glosses, on Suhrawardi's *Hikmat al-ishraq*, and on Qutb al-Din Shirazi's commentary on that text.

17. *Ittihad al-'aqil wa'l-ma'qul*

This is a monographic treatise on the demonstration of a complicated philosophical theory, the Union of the Intellect and the Intelligible, which, prior to Mulla Sadra, no-one had been able to prove and rationalize.

18. *Ajwabah al-masa'il*

This book consists of at least three treatises in which Mulla Sadra responds to the philosophical questions posed by contemporary philosophers.

19. *Ittisaf al-mahiyyah bi'l wujud*

This monographic treatise deals with the problem of existence and its relation to quiddities.

20. *Al-Tashakhkhus*

In this book, Mulla Sadra explains the problem of individuation, and clarifies its relation to existence and its principality (this is one of the most fundamental principles propounded by him).

21. *Sarayan nur wujud*

This treatise deals with the quality of the descent, or diffusion of existence, from the True Source to existents (quiddities).

22. *Limmiyyah ikhtisas al-mintaqah*

A treatise on logic, this work focuses on the cause of the specific form of the sphere.

23. *Khalq al-aʿmal*

This treatise is on man's determinism and free will.

24. *al-Qada' wa'l-qadar*

This treatise is on the problem of Divine Decree and Destiny.

25. *Zad al-musafir*

In this book (which is probably the same as *Zad al-salik*), Mulla Sadra tries to demonstrate resurrection and the Hereafter using a philosophical approach.

26. *Al-Shawahid al-rububiyyah*

This treatise is not related to Mulla Sadra's book *al-Shawahid al-rububiyyah*. It is an inventory of his particular theories and opinions, as he was able to express them in philosophical terms.

27. *al-Mizaj*

Mulla Sadra wrote this treatise on the reality of man's temperament and its relation to the body and soul.

28. *Mutashabihat al-Qur'an*

This treatise consists of Mulla Sadra's interpretations of those Qura'nic verses that have secret and complicated meanings. It is considered to be one of the chapters of *Mafatih al-qayb*.

29. *Isalat-i jaʿl-i wujud*

This book is on existence and its principiality as opposed to quiddities.

30. *Al-Hashriyyah*

A treatise on resurrection and people's presence in the Hereafter, it deals with man's rewards in Paradise and punishment in Hell.

31. *Al-alfad al-mufradah*

This book is used as an abridged dictionary for interpreting words in the Qur'an.

32. *Radd-i shubahat-i Iblis*

Here, Mulla Sadra explains Satan's seven paradoxes and provides appropriate answers.

33. *Sih Asl*

This is Mulla Sadra's only book in Persian. Here, by resorting to the three main moral principles, he deals with moral and educational subjects related to scientists, and advises contemporary philosophers.

34. *Kasr al-asnam al-jahiliyyah*

The title of this book means "demolishing the idols of the periods of barbarism and man's ignorance." His intention here is to condemn and disgrace impious sophists.

35. *Al-Tanqih*

In this book, Mulla Sadra deals concisely with formal logic. It is a good book to use for instruction.

36. *Al-Tasawwur wa'l-tasdiq*

This treatise deals with issues of the philosophy of logic, and enquires into concepts and judgment.

37. *Diwan shi'r* (Collection of Poems)

Mulla Sadra wrote a number of scholarly and mystic poems in Persian, which are compiled in this book.

38. *A Collection of Scientific-Literary Notes*

In his youth, Mulla Sadra studied many philosophical and gnostic books; he was also interested in the work of various poets. This book is a precious collection of juvenilia, and includes some short pieces of his own poetry, the statements of philosophers and gnostics, and discussions of scientific issues. It is said that this book can familiarize the readers with subtleties of Mulla Sadra's nature.

These notes have been compiled in two different collections; it is likely that the smaller collection was compiled on one of his journeys.

39. *Letters*

Except for a few letters exchanged between Mulla Sadra and his master Mir Damad, nothing remains of their correspondence. These letters are included at the beginning of the three-volume book of Mulla Sadra's *Life, Character and School*, written in Persian. This book has also been translated into English.

* * *

If we consider the 39 books listed above, his 12-volume books of interpretation (which we referred to as *Tafasir* [number 2]), *Mafatih al-qayb* and *Asrar al-ayat*, we have cited more than 50 of his works so far. Some other books have also been attributed to him. However, we will not refer to their names; they have either been discussed in other, more comprehensive books, or Mulla Sadra's authorship of them seems unlikely.

There have been many debates around the place and time of composition of Mulla Sadra's books. Most of his books carry no date of composition, which requires the reader to refer to documents and other evidence in order to make estimates. For example, the composition dates of some of his books are implied in his *al-Mabda' wa'l-ma'ad*, *al-Hashr* and in his interpretations of some of the *Surahs* (chapters) of the Qur'an.

For instance, *al-Mabda' wa'l-ma'ad* was written in 1019 AH (1609 AD), *Interpretation of Ayat al-kursi* in about 1023 AH (1613 AD), *Kasr al-asnam* in 1027 AH (1617 AD), *Iksir al-'arifin* in 1031 AH (1621 AD), the treatise of *al-Hashr* in 1032 AH (1622 AD), the treatise of *Ittihad al-'aqil wa'l-ma'qul* in about 1037 AH (1627 AD), and *Mafatih al-qayb* in 1029 AH (1619 AD). The dates of his other books can only be reckoned approximately.

In order to determine their place of composition, we must take into consideration that Mulla Sadra travelled to Qum and its suburbs from Shiraz, or somewhere else, before 1015 AH (1605 AD), and then moved from Qum to Shiraz in about 1040 AH (1630 AD). Therefore, the books that he wrote before 1040 AH must have been written in Qum or somewhere in its vicinity, unless he wrote some of these books and treatises on his long journeys.

The last and most complete edition of this book, along with some critical corrections, has been published by Mulla Sadra Publications Foundation, Tehran, Iran."[9]

40. *The Complete Philosophical Treatises of Mulla Sadra*, ed., Hamid Naji Isfahani, Tehran: Hekmat Publication House, 1996. This book includes 15 short Resaleh, or papers, by him, which were not published or identified until 1996. The papers are titled: *Itihad 'Aqil wa Ma'qul, Ajwabeh Masail Mulla Shamsa Gilani, Ajwabih Masil Mulla Muzafar Hussein Kashani, Ajwabih Masail Nasyriiih, Risalih Asalat Ja'l Wujud, Risalih Tanqih dar Mantiq, Risalih Hashryyeh, Risalih Khalsih, Dibajih 'Arsh al-Taqdis, Risalih Khalq al-A'amal, Risalih Shawahid al-Rububyyih,* Fawaid *(Rad Shubahat Iblisyyih, Sharh Hadith Kuntu Kanzan Makhfya, Dar Bayan Kayfat Tarkib, Madih wa Surat, Zei Ayeh Amanat wa Mawad Thalath), Risalih Lemyyah Dar Ikhtisas Falak, Risalih Mizaj, Tafsir Surih Tawhid (1), Tafsir Surih Tawhid(2), Risalih Wujud, Risalih Hall Shubhiyyh Jazr Asam.*

41. *Mathnawi Mulla Sadra*, ed. Mustafa Fayzi, Qum, 1376.

The Style of His Writings:

On the whole, Sadr al-Muta'llihIn's books can be classified into two categories:

a. Written with the aim of explaining a subject under study and examining the results of its proofs, but without mention of any differences of opinions on the subject or the proofs thereof.
b. Written with the aim of logically providing proofs and expounding on subjects that have inspired debate, and from which different views have emerged, E.g. *al-Asfar al-Arba'ah* and the *Sharh al-Usul min al-Kafi*.

The aim of the second category is to enable the reader to attain the desired goal; the author adopts a practical approach and conducts the reader step by step to the intended goal. Hence, in the beginning he introduces a subject the way it is discussed in the popular texts, mentions the variety of opinions and views on the subject, and then discusses the proofs provided by its proponents and opponents. Afterwards, he criticizes them and exposes the fallacies in their arguments, but first warns that engaging in such a pursuit is not necessary.

"It is not the norm for the seekers of truth to bother with the views of those who lack intuition and insight into the realities of the cosmos—these misguided individuals, like the majority of theologians, linguists and rhetoricians. But there is no harm in mentioning their views, elucidating the meaning of their words, and defining the limits of their concepts, from which we can derive underlying principles and extract the truth of the matter."[10]

Finally, he discloses his specialist view and proceeds to elaborate and prove it.

"So let us mention the criticism that is leveled against it by the opponents of Forms. We will point out those aspects which are familiar to the researching minds, and then we shall return to what God has shown us of its proofs, disclosing to our psyches and opening to our hearts the door of His Mercy and Pleasure. Thus, we shall reveal a portion of it and not shy away from expressing the truth, even though it may disagree with the popular view."[11]

In a letter to his teacher, Mir Damad, he writes:

"There are many profound issues and subtle realities which have been unveiled for this humble soul and defective intellect, most of which are extremely unfamiliar to the popular contemporary thinking. Though we have established clear logical proofs for them and they are not beyond the scope of the discursive method, they are unknown to the temperaments of the majority of the theology students and intellectuals; hence, we have not explicitly stated them in our writings. Thus, we have made passing remarks regarding some of the views, while others we have scattered and presented in between detailed discussions wherein we exposed them to purified minds and sharp intellects. However, what is embedded deep in our thoughts has not been written."[12]

"Those familiar with subtleties have more to say but cannot express it explicitly, since ordinary minds will fail to comprehend it and the degenerate will stand in opposition."[13]

"Let us hold back ourselves from elaboration. In fact, the reins of control over speech have been loosened and what has been mentioned is beyond the comprehension of ordinary minds and intellects."[14]

It has been difficult for the educated to distinguish his views from other opinions. One cannot comprehend them until one studies his works more generally (especially those written in the last years of his honorable life), scrutinizes them, and delves into their depths. On occasion, he quotes others' views and arguments on a subject without explicitly stating his own unique view:

"And we have discussed in detail, but there still remain some hidden aspects in the corners of our heart—to elaborate on the issue and elucidate the matter—which we have foregone since space does not permit . . . There is a strong dissuading factor present, while a powerful persuasive factor is absent; namely, the inability to comprehend these issues by the ordinary student and the abomination of the degenerate ones—the latter being slothful and ignorant in their approach."[15]

"And the philosopher does not bother about the popular views and is not concerned about the majority's opinions if he has attained the truth. And in every topic he does not focus on who says what, but rather on what is said."[16]

Another of Sadra's tendencies is to quote the views and opinions of his predecessors without specifying his sources. This style of presentation has made him the target of criticism by narrow-minded opponents who accuse him of plagiarism without taking note of his published views on the issue of attribution:

"This is all that the author of *al-Mutaharat* has mentioned from the ancient scholars. We have quoted [it] verbatim, because I found no benefit in altering the phrases, since the purpose is to convey the meaning with whatever words"[17]

"This is all that we intended to mention in this key (*Miftah*). We have preferred to merely quote what other scholars of Islam have mentioned on this issue, avoiding spending more time searching for better words and forms, since the purpose was to express similar ideas and meanings."[18]

At times he employs the tactic of quoting supporting evidence for his views from the writings of the ancient philosophers, while interpreting their views to conform to his own:

"We have, in dealing with this important issue, relied not only on the views of the ancient scholars but also on logical proofs; though if their views are seen to conform with ours, the heart is more satisfied."[19]

His Poetry:

Mulla Sadra is not really a poet, but he has composed some poetry.

The only known poetry of Sadr al-Muta'lihin is "Muntakhab al-Mathnavi" which was printed as an appendix to his treatise *Sih Asl* along with his quartets. However he also quotes some of his poetry in between his writings. He writes in the introduction to Surah al-Sajdah:

"I had composed some poetry in Persian in praise of the Holy Quran and its status as spiritual sustenance whose consumption is exclusive to human souls steeped in divine love. I have mentioned some of those here . . ."[20]

Also: "I had composed some poetry on this theme when I experienced an expansiveness in my heart and disclosure in my soul . . ."[21]

And in the commentary on Ayah al-Nur he writes:

"And there is a garden from the gardens of Paradise within you, inasmuch as there is a pit from the pits of the Hell-fire within you. As I have mentioned in the Mathnavi: Darooni buwad rawzai az behesht . . ." [22]

Recently his *Matnawi*, which consists of 2150 verses in *bahr raml* style, like Rumi's *Mathnawi*, was edited by Mustafa Fayzi and published by Ketabkhanih Ayatullah Mar'ashi Najafi in Qum, 1376.

Endnotes:

1. There is a difference of opinion about Mulla Sadra's year of death. All his biographers mention it as 1050 A.H./1640 C.E., notes from his grandson, Allamah 'Alam al-Huda—who quotes from the notes of his own father, Mulla Muhammad Mushin Faiz Kashani—indicate that the year of his death was actually 1045 A.H. One thing we can be sure about is that he lived up to 1037 A.H., as indicated in the introduction to his treatise entitled "The Book of Metaphysical Penetrations" (*Al-Masha'ir*), in which he writes: "It *(this book)* has been completed on Friday afternoon, the 7th of Jamadi al-Awwal 1037 A.H. This is while the writer has passed 58 years of his life." It appears the two dates can be reconciled with the explanation that Mulla Sadra died in 1045 A.H. in Basra but his remains were transferred to Najaf in 1050 A.H., since 'Alam al-Huda quotes his father that he, Faiz Kashani, visited the grave of his teacher in the right chamber of the holy shrine of Imam Ali ('a).
2. Rumi, Book III of *Mathnawi*, Verses 2648-2654.
3. Mulla Sadra, *Montakhab Mathnawi, enzemam resaleh sih asl.*
4. Mulla Sadra, *Asfar*, vol 1, p. 6.
5. Mulla Sadra, *al-Mabda wa al-M'aad*, p. 382.
6. Mulla Sadra, *Tafsir ayat al-kursi*: p. 60.
7. Mulla Sadra, *Asrar al-ayat*: p. 181.
8. Mulla Sadra, *Asfar*, vol. 1, p. 6.
9. http://www.mullasadra.org/new_site/english/mullasadra/works.htm
10. Mulla Sadra, *Mafatih al-Ghaib*, p. 99.
11. Mulla Sadra, *Asfar*, vol1, p.85.
12. *Farhang Iran Zamin*, vol 13, p 94.
13. Mulla Sadra, *al-Tafsir*, vol2, p 173.
14. Mulla Sadra, *Mafatih al-Ghayb*, p. 351.
15. Mulla Sadra, *Tafsir Sureh Yasin*, p. 256.
16. (Mulla Sadra, *Asfar*, vol6, p.6.
17. Mulla Sadra, *Asfar*, vol5, p.174.
18. Mulla Sadra, *Mafatih al-Ghayb*, p. 317.
19. Mulla Sadra, *Asfar*, vol5, p.300.
20. Mulla Sadra, *Surah al-Sajdah*, p. 9.
21. Ibid, p. 34.
22. Mulla Sadra, *Tafsir Ayah al-Nur*, p. 408.

Mulla Sadra's Transcendent Philosophy

Introduction:

This chapter discusses the philosophy of Mulla Sadra, one of the most important Muslim Iranian philosophers and founder of new school of Islamic philosophy, entitled Transcendent philosophy, in 3 sections:, what is the "Transcendent philosophy", the 16 principles of Mulla Sadra's philosophy and Mulla Sadra's views on different schools of thought such as Ancient Metaphysicians, Greek and Muslim philosophers, and *'Urafa*, This is an original paper in the English language as it presents the most important aspects of Mulla Sadra's philosophy based directly on his various writings in Arabic language, such as *Asfar, al-Shawahid al-rububiyya, al-Mabda' wa l-Ma'ad, Arshiyyah, al-Masha'ir* and *Mafatih al-Ghayb*.

1. *Al-Hikmah* (Theosophy) and Transcendent Philosophy[1]

Hikmah (theosophy) is the understanding of Existence by Divine intelligence. The knowledge of Almighty God is the most supreme of all kinds of knowledge, and concerns the best of what can be known. ˉSadr al-Muta'llihin believes that engaging oneself with other kinds of knowledge is to prefer the inferior to the superior. As long as there exist those who are capable of engaging themselves in particular sciences and worldly knowledge, which is the case in every place and in every epoch, it does not behoove an intellectual to occupy himself with these matters, thus overlooking superior and sacred knowledge.

Therefore you will find that most of Mulla Sadra's books, not excepting *al-Asfar al-Arba'ah*, were based on this kind of knowledge. Whenever he mentioned a matter pertaining to another discipline, he would usually alert the reader to the link between the two:

"And since I do not like a Divine personality to refer to one who is learned [merely] in the particular sciences, whether it be matters concerning natural sciences or otherwise . . . For this reason, I have not included the references in most of the places of the commentary of the present book, but have placed them as a part of the original text, as is my normal habit in my magnum opus called Al-Asfar which consists of four volumes, all of which pertain to metaphysics in its two parts: primary philosophy and the art of separate substances."[2]

"It was a traditional norm to mention this issue in the discipline of natural sciences. However, we have included it here for the aforementioned reason and for the reason that the discussion on the quiddity of a thing, and the nature of its existence, is suitable in a discussion of the divine disciplines."[3]

Transcendent Philosophy

Transcendent philosophy focuses attention on spiritual vision and intuition and thus surpasses conventional theosophy. Mulla Sadra was of the opinion that gnosis can be attained in three ways:

1) Intellectual proof
2) Spiritual vision
3) Divine revelation.

The intellect finds itself incompetent in transcendent, divine discussions, because it knows of a realm beyond its own realm. Thus the path of success is that of spiritual vision, endorsed by Revelation which is not inconsistent, nor contrary to reliable intellectual proof. This is the basis depended upon in the Transcendental philosophy, from which Mulla Sadra took the name for his *magnum opus, al-Asfar al-Arba'ah*. He adopts this method of understanding in most of his subtle discussions.

Avicenna was probably the first person to employ the term "transcendent theosophy," when he said:

"Then, if what it implies is a kind of opinion that is hidden save to those well-rooted in the transcendent theosophy (al-Hikmat al-muta`liyah)."[4]

In his commentary on the *al-Isharat*, Muhaqiq Tusi says:

"Surely he only considered this issue to be one of transcendent theosophy because the Peripatetic philosophy is a mere discursive theosophy, while this issue and its likes are properly elucidated by means of discourse together with spiritual vision and intuition. Thus, the philosophy that includes these methods of understanding is relatively superior (*muta`;liyah*) to the first kind of theosophy."[5]

Qaysari, the commentator of *Fusus*, had also used this term:

"And the difference between the two is similar to the difference between the universal and its two particulars and not like the difference between two distinct realities, as those who have no knowledge of the transcendental theosophy surmise."[6]

Some of the secrets of religion are of a level that is beyond intellectual thought, and can only be understood by the light of Sainthood and Prophethood. The relation between the realm of the intellect and its light, and the realm of Sainthood and its light, is analogous to the relation between the light of the senses and the light of the intellect. Thus there is not much benefit in the application of the intellect to this realm that is beyond its reach.

In the introduction to his commentary on Chapter *Al-Waqi'ah* of the Holy Qur'an, Mulla Sadra explains how he arrived at this path of understanding:

"And in the past I frequently engaged in discourse and reiteration and often occupied myself in studying the books of far-sighted philosophers, until I thought I had gained something. But when my inner vision opened a little and I looked at my own state, I found that, although I had attained knowledge of the disciplines of reality, matters pertaining to the Source of being, His transcendence over contingent and ephemeral attributes, and the Return of the human soul to Absolute Truth could not be comprehended save through intuition and spiritual experience. And these matters also exist in the Book of Allah and the Sunnah, e.g. the Gnosis of God, His Attributes and Names, etc. the reality of which cannot be known save through Allah's guidance, and cannot be unraveled save by the light of Prophethood and Sainthood.

And the difference between the knowledge of far-sighted intellectuals and the knowledge of those possessing insight is like the difference between knowing the definition of sweetness and [literally] tasting the same. Therefore I became convinced that these realities of faith could not be comprehended save by means of cleansing the heart of vain desires, purifying it of mundane motives, and isolating oneself from the masses, especially the clever among them; and by means of contemplating the Qur'anic verses and the tradition of the Prophet Muhammad (S) and following the path of the virtuous for the rest of one's short life span: before us lies a long journey. Hence when I felt my weakness, I was sure that I had not yet attained anything. [Instead] I had satisfied myself with the shadow rather than the ray of light . . . My soul lit up powerfully in my extreme plight, and my heart burnt with the light of extreme restlessness. As a result, the Eternal and Abundant Mercy of God embraced it and Divine Grace turned towards it with flashes from the spiritual realm, and thereby graced it from His fathomless ocean of generosity with some of the mysteries of existence. And the Revealer of the secrets and the Luminant of quiddities bestowed upon me some of the secrets of His signs and palpable divine visions."[7]

"For surely I believe in the truth of all that our Prophet Muhammad (S) brought and the truth of the prophethood of prophet Musa ('a) as well. And this is not due to the miracle of splitting the moon or transforming the rod into a serpent, but by divine indications and divine inspirations in the heart, which do not allow any speck of skepticism or doubt and are not afflicted by any stain of obscurity and defect. Nonetheless, they are measured and comprehended correctly by the balances of justice of the Day of Reckoning, a measure that Allah brought down from the Heaven of pure intelligence to the earthly human heart located below the heaven of the elevated intellect, and He commanded us to keep it upright, as the following verses of the Holy Qur'an manifest: '. . . and the heaven—He raised it up, and set the Balance, therefore weigh with justice, and skimp not in the balance. And the earth—He set it down for all beings." (Quran, 55:7-10). And indeed I kept this correct balance upright as Allah ordered to be done, and I measured all the divine matters. Rather, [I also measured] the states of the Return in the Hereafter and . . . I found all of them in conformity with what exists in this Qur'an. Also, I became convinced of the fact that all the authentic traditions of the Holy Prophet Muhammad (S) are veracious and the truth."[8]

Some pertinent issues on the relationship between the intellect and Revelation:

1) Mulla Sadra does not invalidate intellectual judgment, nor does he oust it from the realm of gnosis. Rather he believes that:

"It is inadmissible for one to comprehend in the realm of spiritual vision what the intellect believes to be impossible. Nevertheless, it is possible for a thing that is beyond the intellectual grasp to appear in the realm of spiritual vision. In other words, the intellect is inadequate to comprehend it. One who cannot differentiate between that which the intellect believes to be impossible and that which the intellect cannot comprehend is not eligible to be addressed. Hence he should be left alone with his ignorance."[9]

2) The means of distinguishing what the intellect finds to be correct and not contradicting the truth is Revelation. Hence no impartial and correct kind of philosophy can transgress what it says. *"Indeed what else is beyond the truth save aberration"* (Holy Qur'an 10:32).

"And one whose religion is not that of the Prophets ('a), that is not considered to be theosophy at all. And one who is not firmly rooted in the gnosis of realities is not considered to be from the theosophists." [10]

However, in the manner of convincing intellectual proof, neither does the follower of the Prophet (s.a.w.) reject the judgment made by the intellect:

"And how can one who is merely satisfied in accepting the traditions with no proof, and who negates the methods of thought and intellection, attain guidance? Doesn't he know that there is no reliable source for religion save the speech of the master of mankind, and the intellect that assents to the truth of what he reported? Also, how can one who merely adopts intellectual proof and satisfies himself thereby but has not yet been illuminated by the light of religion, be guided to the truth? I wish I knew how one may seek refuge in the intellect, when it is afflicted by incapacitation and limitation? Doesn't he realize that the intellect is incapable of comprehending [some of] the realities until it is illuminated by the light of religion, and that its bounds are very narrow?"

"How far-fetched! How far-fetched! Surely one who does not harmonize religion and intellectual judgment in this manner is definitely lacking. For the example of the intellect is eyesight free from calamities and maladies and the example of the Holy Qur'an is a Sun whose light-rays are spread out. Therefore it is appropriate to consider that that seeker of guidance, who finds himself satisfied with one instead of both of the sources of comprehension, is one of the unwise [and narrow-minded]. Similarly, he who shuns the intellect and limits himself to the light of the Holy Qur'an and the traditions of the Prophet and his progeny ('a) is one who enjoys the presence of the light of the Sun and the Moon, but shuts his eyelids. Thus there is no difference between him and the blind. Therefore religion together with the intellect is light upon light."[11]

"And it is far-fetched for the laws of the true brilliant religion to contradict the definite teachings [comprehended by the intellect]. And may the philosophy whose laws are not in conformity with the Book of God and the Sunnah of the Prophet (S) be vanquished."[12]

3) There is another path for attaining divine realities, which has no parallel. For that which is heard is not like that which is beheld in its entirety and that is veracious spiritual vision. Hence, even though the scholars reckon that they can attain the realities on this path, this is unlikely due to the arduousness of the path and the difficulty of the practice. The beholder is optimistic due to the loftiness of what he would attain and the composure he would experience thereby:

"And the reality of theosophy is only gotten from divinely gifted knowledge. And as long as the soul has not attained this station, he will not be a theosopher."[13]

If prophetic intuition is intuition which has not a speck of doubt, then religion is the scale by which to measure other intuitions; and therefore that vision which does not conform to it has no weight:

"Surely I seek refuge with my Sublime Lord in all my statements, acts, beliefs and writings, from all that contradicts the truth of following the religion brought by the doyen of the Messengers of Allah and the Seal of the Prophets, upon whom and whose progeny be the best felicitations of the felicitators."[14]

That which the Beholder comprehends through intuition cannot be elucidated and proved for any other than the beholder save by means of intellectual proof. Thus, the possessor of knowledge of transcendental theosophy comprehends intellectually and intuitively, and agrees with what the religion has to say.

"Our statements should not be considered to be merely the result of spiritual vision and intuition or assimilation of religion without understanding the intellectual proofs and observing its laws. For indeed mere intuition without intellectual ratification is insufficient for wayfaring, inasmuch as mere discourse without spiritual vision is a great defect in wayfaring . . .

We have repeatedly pointed out that theosophy does not contradict the veracious divine religions. Rather, the aim behind both is one and the same: the gnosis of the Foremost Truth, His Attributes and . . . His Acts. And these are sometimes attained through spiritual wayfaring and acquisition, and therefore such comprehension is known as theosophy and spiritual sanctity (*wilayah*). And only one who has no knowledge of how to harmonize religious addresses with intellectual proofs believes them to be in contradiction. And none can do that save one who is backed by Allah, perfect in intellectual disciplines, and aware of the prophetic mysteries. For verily there may be a person who is proficient in discursive theosophy, but has no share of the knowledge of the Book of God and religion, and conversely."[15]

Mulla Sadra's ingenuity comes to the fore in this field, for, through his efforts, the travails of the theosophers, who had struggled to intellectually prove the gnosis, reached perfection through spiritual vision and intuition.

"And indeed we harmonized their intuitions with intellectual principles."[16]

"And I suppose that, in spite of the fact that the words of the ancient scholars explained these issues, and in spite of the fact that the statements of the researchers meant to express them, nevertheless, none had produced such intellectual proofs based on principles that had confused [even] the intellects of the far-sighted scholars."[17]

Mulla Sadra believes that one who has no hope of traversing the spiritual path will not benefit by studying his books. He says:

"Therefore understand if you rank among those who can appreciate [the teachings]. If not, then stop reading this book and contemplating the abstruse issues of the knowledge of Qur'an. Instead, you should pursue the knowledge of anecdotes, reports, traditions and the science of history and genealogy, and get acquainted with Arabic and language and accept traditions without any in-depth understanding, and acquire the conclusions you make from all the aforesaid sciences that deal with controversial secondary issues."[18]

"And it is prohibited for most people to start acquiring these abstruse disciplines, because those who are capable of comprehending them are extremely scarce. And the ability to comprehend them is bestowed by Allah, the Invincible and All-knowledgeable."[19]

"And I had no intention in proving every issue save guiding the astute student and cleansing the pure mind, who will thereby attain the nearness of Allah and his exalted spiritual realm. Thus if this corresponds with the opinion of the people of discourse and scrutiny, it will be as we have indicated. But if it does not correspond with their opinion, then it is known that truth is not in compatible with the intellects of a people whose dispositions have been destroyed by inner maladies that the spiritual doctors have been unable to cure . . . And a Divine theosophist should not engage in any kind of conversation with those people, nor write for them nor call and address them."[20]

2. Principles of Mulla Sadra's Transcendental Philosophy[21]

1- Principality of Existence and Its Unity[22]

We only perceive something as a single entity in the outside realm. However, the intellect divides it into quiddity (*mahiyyah*) and existence (*wujud*). But which of these is fundamental and principal in the outside realm?

This question had not been discussed with much clarity among the ancient philosophers. And as such, we may find areas in their works that sometimes reveal that existence is fundamental and, at other times, that quiddity is fundamental (*asil*). The belief in the fundamentality of quiddity was first introduced to us by Shaykh al-Ishraq and later garnered acceptance among some theosophers, such as Mir Damad.

At first, Mulla Sadra, too, adopted this notion, following in the footsteps of his teacher, Mir Damad. However, later when the reality was unraveled for him he started to believe in the fundamentality of existence, instead. He was so firmly confident in the idea that he made it the foremost principle, and the foundational stone, of nearly all of his philosophical proofs.

"And I used to highly support them in their belief that Existence is derivative (*i'tibari*) and that quiddities are fundamental (*asil*) until my Lord guided me and the opposite was clearly unraveled for me: that 'existents' are principal realities in the outside realm."[23]

The notion of the fundamentality of existence was also well known among Islamic Gnostics even believed by some. However, it was not intellectually proven in the manner propounded in the transcendental theosophy.

After arguing for the principality of Existence, the intellects then propounded its singleness. This forms the second principle upon which nearly all other metaphysical issues depend.

The Gnostics, indeed, used to believe in the hypostatic unity *(wahdah shakhsiyyah)* of existence and, at times, even tried to prove it in order to counter the vehemence of its opponents. However, they lacked any real success in demonstrating firm intellectual proofs to back their claims. Their body of evidence, rather, was as limited as those of the theologians who were not immune to criticisms, imperfections and weaknesses themselves.

We must be alert of the fact that Mulla Sadra first propounded the particular unity of existence and its gradational characteristic, providing the establishment upon which the solution to other problems depended. Then, he arrived at a deeper understanding, which is the belief in the hypostatic unity of existence supported by the mystics. It is apparent in many of his works that he supports their opinion.

After realizing that his claims found disapproval among the masses and started arousing opposition, he propounded the idea of the particular unity of existence and walked on its path, breaking the vehemence of those opponents and safeguarding himself from the condemnation of the ignorant and the pseudo-philosophers. Alluding to the truth and the more subtle opinion he espoused, he made the following point:

"Indeed, it is understood from the statements of the intellectual who possesses the power of intuition (¦ads) what we are in the process of ratifying when its time comes. And that is the fact that all contingent existents and suspended copulative entities (*al-inniyyat al-irtibatiyyah al-ta`alluqiyyah*) are manifestations of the Necessary Existent and the rays and shadows of the light of ontic Sovereignty . . . Therefore, the reality is One and the rest are none, save for its manifestations, the rays of its light, the shadows of its rays, and the manifestations of its Essence.

And by Allah's grace and support, I have demonstrated a brilliant proof for this lofty and sacred contention, written in a separate treatise on this subject called, *"Tarhu'l Kawnayn"*—a proof that is subtle, desired, and invaluable. And God-Willing, we shall place it in its respective area of discussion as we promised." [24]

"And this principle is of the principles that establish what we are in the process of ratifying; and that is the fact that all the [contingent] entities in view of their nature of existence are the overflows, emanations, and flakes of the Divine Existence—they are the manifestations and theophanies of the Infinite Truth."[25]

He fulfills his promise to demonstrate the proof in his first book (*"safar"* literally meaning "journey"), where he proves the transcendent hypostatic unity of existence after relating effect-hood (*ma'luliyyah*) to trait-hood (*tasha'un*). Then, in a state of joy, he says:

And the proof for this principle is of the wisdom that my Lord bestowed on me by His Eternal Grace and made it my share of knowledge by the bestowal of the Grace of His Existence. Thus, through this principle I tried to perfect philosophy and complete theosophy.

And since this principle is subtle, abstruse, and has shown to be difficult to follow and comprehend—and particularly because its ascertainment is far-reaching—most theosophers overlooked it and the feet of many students slipped in negligence, not to mention that of their followers, imitators, and associates.

And in the manner that my Lord enabled me through His Grace and Mercy to comprehend the perpetual annihilation and eternal extinction of the contingent quiddities, He guided me through a brilliant proof to the straight path of truth: the fact that existence is confined to one hypostatic reality, which has no partner in the reality of existence and where there is no second to it in essence."[26]

Hence, there is a difference in the way of understanding between the seer who beholds the universe as a collection of different quiddities, each of which is independent of the other, and a philosopher who through deep insight comprehends it to be harmonious, interrelated, and one in which Allah is the light of the heavens and the earth.

2- Trans-Substantial Motion

All the theosophers believed in the occurrence of trans-substantial motion in some of the accidental categories *(maqulat al-'araziyyah)*, but due to difficulties (primarily the obscurity of the discontinuity of the subject) they were reluctant in accepting such motion in the category of substance *(maqulat al-jawhar)*.

"And the later theosophists, such as Abu 'Ali and his likes, were extremely persistent in denying this substantial transformation. And that is why they were unable to prove many true concepts..."[27]

The most distinctive notion that Mulla Sadra introduced is the belief in trans-substantial motion and the responses of the obscurities that it is confronted with. Although this principle was inspired by the belief of the mystics in the renewal of *amthal*, the difference in the two ideas is apparent. Furthermore, the belief in *amthal* was not intellectually proven by Gnostics.

He is the first to consider and support the idea of trans-substantial motion. In addition, he relied on it to solve a number of other issues.

"And that which we have gotten through power from the exalted celestial realm (and not by studying the heritage of the theosophers) is that motion takes place in substance and the nature of specific bodies are perpetually in a state of renewal and change in their essence..."[28]

Indeed, it is impossible to harmonize between theosophy and religion in the temporal genesis of the world and understand the fact that it has no beginning, except through this principle. And 'Allamah Tabatabaei in his gloss on the Asfar says:

"And the truth is that the belief in the occurrence of movement in the category of substance necessitates its occurrence in all the [other] categories. And although the author stressed its occurrence in the category of substance and tried to explain and prove the same in his books, he did not present a complete discussion by minding to include the branches of this important issue that transform divine philosophy into a new invaluable basis. In-spite of this, he has done a great favor to the philosophers of this issue."[29]

3- Temporal Createdness of The Material World

Ever since the olden times, this matter was under question among theosophers and theologians. The theosophers, relying on the Emanation of the Necessary Being and the impossibility of the occurrence of change in His Essence, prefer to believe that He possesses Eternal Emanation. Contrarily, the theologians for fear that this notion could lead to the belief that the world does not need a cause and that it would itself transform into a Necessary Being—negate this belief and consider it to be infidelity and heresy. Furthermore, they allege that all the monotheistic nations are unanimous in its opposition.

Perhaps hearing the words, "eternal" *(al-qadim)* and "continual" *(al-dawam)* with regards to that other than the Necessary Existent is what provokes such contestation. Thus, the following passage, taken from a section of *"Mafatih al-Ghayb,"* can be regarded as controversial. In it, Mulla Sadra states:

"A section dealing with the fact that motion, in view of its temporal genesis, manifests continual and endless movement. And proving this is of the things that provoke a group of insane proponents of folklore because its apparent import manifests the pre-eternity of the world . . . However, we are in the process of proving temporal created-ness."[30]

Some have attempted to harmonize the two above mentioned statements, including Mir Damad, Mulla Sadra's teacher in metaphysics, who introduced him to the idea of "atemporal created-ness" *(al-huduth al-dahri)* and on the same subject wrote a book entitled, *"Al-Qabasat."* He also wrote a treatise on the "temporal created-ness of the world." Nevertheless, Mulla Sadra, his student, utilizing a belief in trans-substantial motion, propounded another view and proved as fact that the material world is perpetually contingent and "coming into being" and, therefore, can never be eternal and necessary. For this very reason, he wrote a separate treatise on the temporal created-ness of the world, which he mentions and gives reference to in most of his books.

"Indeed we taught and guided you to the celestial path which none of the theosophers—well-known for their skillful ability to prove the temporality of the material world, including all that it embraces of the heavens and the earth—had done before . . .

Know the fact that this is from the greatest issues of belief and gnosis, and all the prophetic religions have unanimously agreed on its establishment, while its comprehension eludes the bewildered intellects of the theosophers. And surely, Allah has inspired us to understand this issue by the virtue of his Beneficence and has thereby preferred us over many of his other creations."[31]

And he is extremely happy in having solved this issue when he says:

"Know the fact that the elucidation of this aspiration and the realization of this statement—which echoes the successive and famously narrated tradition of the Prophet (S) that says, "Allah Existed while there was nothing with Him"—is of those abstruse matters, the particular information of which neither I, at sixty five years of age, nor anyone else on the face of this earth, have found within a lifetime. Also, I did not find proof on this matter that cures the sick and satiates the thirsty in books of the ancient and succeeding scholars. Surely, Allah advantaged me through His Mercy and Grace, and opened the door of comprehending its truth in my heart. As a result, I placed this sublime issue, along with unique and magnificent pearls of wisdom, in some of my books and treatises."[32]

This shows that the matter was controversial among the thinkers of his time and the treatises written on the issue by his contemporaries explains why Sadr al-Muta'allihin laid importance on it. There exists a hand written manuscript of the treatise which Mulla Sadra wrote and sent to Shams al-Jilani.

4- Union Of The Intelligent And The Intelligible

This notion was well known from ancient scholars and perfect Gnostics. However, its expurgation and exposition in the form of a specific intellectual proof was first introduced by Mulla Sadra:

"Surely, the notion of the soul comprehending the forms of intelligible entities is of the most abstruse problems of theosophy that none among the Islamic scholars has expurgated and propounded immaculately until today. We found the difficult nature of this issue and contemplated the problem of the knowledge of substance being itself a substance and an accident. We also did not find in the books of the philosophers (not excepting their president Ibn Sina, such as al-Shifa, al-Najat, al-Isharat, and 'Uyun al-Hikmah and others) that which cures the sick and satiates the thirsty. Rather, we found that he and all those at his level, his likes, his followers, such as his student, Bahmanyar, and the master of the followers of the stoics, and Muhaqqiq Tusi Nasir al-Din, and other posterior philosophers, failed to bring something dependable ... Thus, we naturally turned to the Cause of All the Means and expressed our intrinsic humiliation to the Simplifier of difficulties and asked Him to open the door of understanding the reality of this matter ... Thus, during the hour in which I was engaged in writing this section, He Bestowed on us new knowledge from the treasury of His Knowledge." [33]

It is well known that Ibn Sina negated this notion and refuted it with numerous drawbacks. And in his book, *al-Isharat*, *namat* ninth, after mentioning the refutations, he reproachfully says:

"And among them was a person known as Prophyry who had written a book on intellect and intelligible entities, which the Peripatetic philosophers praised when it was entirely unsubstantial! And they themselves know that neither them, nor Prophyry himself understands it ... ."

Thereupon Mulla Sadra replies to his refutations and expounds the unsubstantial areas of his statements, utilizing this principle in expounding many issues.

"Surely, it is my unique finding based on principles that I have established. For verily, it is the final word whose understanding the laymen cannot attain, since it is an elevated cliff and a sacred aspiration, and to understand it requires a second, or rather a third, disposition." [34]

5- Knowledge of Allah[35]

Of the intricate issues concerning Divine Unity is the Knowledge of God about that other than Himself. Mulla Sadra in his al-Asfar al-Arba'ah mentions seven opinions concerning this issue and, thereafter, refutes all of them comprehensively. He proves the knowledge of Allah through the principle that says: "the Truth in its simplicity contains all things" *(basit al-haqaqah kull al-ashya')*. He says:

"Therefore this is the zenith of research on this issue. And perhaps there is no book that has proved this matter before this one. Then O you who are contemplating over it, understand its priceless value and join this precious gem with its likes that are scattered."[36]

Although he attributed the path that he adapted to the ancient well-rooted theosophers, and it nearly tallies with what the perfect Gnostics believed, this exposition was not known before him as he clearly states after expounding the method of the Gnostics:

"However, due to their complete attention towards what they practiced in terms of spiritual austerities, and their inexperience in rational demonstrations and intellectual arguments, perhaps they could not express their ideas and establish their spiritual disclosures in the form of teaching."[37]

In his commentary on the *al-Kafi* he says:

"And this issue is exactly like that of existence; each of them is like the other. Moreover, neither did I find anyone on the face of the earth who had knowledge of any of these matters, nor did I come across [even] one statement that proved and accurately demonstrated this issue in any of the books of the theosophers and scholars . . ."[38]

Some scholars were of the opinion that this notion was not yet perfectly established in his view when he wrote his book, *"al-Mabda' wa al-Ma'ad"* because he had not expounded it as usual. However, what seems more plausible is that which he alluded to in his *"al-Shawahid al-Rububiyyah,"* where he says:

"The object of His perfect knowledge about contingent beings is neither what the Peripatetic philosophers believed . . . nor is it what Plato held . . . nor is it what was held to be true in the hearts of the posterior philosophers. Rather, it is how Allah taught me through a specific way different from the aforementioned ways; and I do not see any benefit in quoting the same due to its intricacy and the difficulty for many minds to comprehend it." [39]

6- Truth in Its Simplicity Contains All Things

Although this principle was inherited from the ancient scholars, its exposition and application in solving various issues concerning monotheism, especially the issue of the knowledge of the Necessary Existent, is of the inventions of Mulla Sadra.

"Truly the reality of the Necessary Being is extremely Simple. And every reality that is Simple is, thus, all the things. Therefore, the Necessary Being is all things and none of the things is beyond His Existence . . ."[40]

"This is among the abstruse Divine issues, the comprehension of which is difficult, save for one whom Allah has endowed with knowledge and wisdom. Nevertheless, there exists intellectual proof for the fact that every simple reality is equal to all existent entities, save for that which is related to imperfections and nonentities . . ."[41]

7- *Platonic Ideas*

Platonic ideas (*muthul*) or archetypes (*arbab al-anwa'*) had been controversial among the scholars since olden times. Plato was the first person to believe in this idea, while Aristotle did not accept it. This notion is considered to be the agent of separation between the two philosophers. Thereafter, peripatetic philosophers from the followers of Aristotle persisted in its negation and Ibn Sina in his al-Shifa' (Shifa, Ilahiyyat, article 7, sections 2&3) propounded his own refutation against it. Shaykh Ishraq, however, adopted it, and in his *Hikmat al-Ishraq* said:

"The writer was a firm supporter of the path of the peripatetic philosophers in negating these things. And were he not to comprehend the proof of his Lord, he would be persistent in his support of this notion . . ."[42]

Mulla Sadra agreed with Plato's notion and said:

"And surely, we have proved this great notion and supported his grand teachers in a manner that does not accept contradictions and refutations."[43]

Mulla Sadra believes that:

"It was not easy for any philosopher that came after the ancient epoch to prove this notion and expurgate it from invectives and doubts, save for one from this blessed nation."[44]

"And I do not know if anyone who came after a great personality of his likes throughout these lengthy ages has attained, through intellectual conviction, the understanding of what he meant, save for one unknown and isolated destitute." [45]

Concerning this issue Mulla Sadra believes that:

"Surely, for every material species there exists a perfect and complete example in the world of Divine Command, which is the root and the origin. And the rest of the species are its offshoots and effects. The reason for this is its completeness and perfection, and the fact that it does not need matter or place. Contrarily, the material species, due to its feebleness and imperfection, needs matter in its essence or action."[46]

8- Soul Is Materially Temporal And Spiritually Subsistent [47]

This subject of how the soul came into existence has been under discussion since olden times. Two popular opinions are:

- One was that of Plato who believed in its pre-eternity
- Other was that of Aristotle who believed in its temporal genesis.

Every philosophical school of thought accepted one of the two notions.

The refutations that confronted the first opinion kept the intellectuals from accepting it. On the other hand, there were numerous traditions on the creation of souls prior to bodies that prevented one from accepting the second opinion, also. Furthermore, there is another difficult question that must be answered and that is the manner in which the body influences the soul in spite of the latter being immaterial in nature.

Extensive struggle on this issue was met with no success until Mulla Sadra came and propounded his famous opinion that the soul is materially temporal and spiritually subsistent, and that the fact that the cause in its existential degree includes the existence of the effect removes the contradiction of the pre-eternal existence of the soul together with its temporal genesis.

"However, those firmly rooted in knowledge who harmonize intellectual proof and spiritual vision believe that the soul possesses numerous degrees of existence and, in spite of its simplicity, has existential modes some of which are above the world of matter, some together with the world of matter, and others beyond the world of matter. And they found that the human souls exist prior to their bodies according to the perfect nature of its cause and means. And a perfect means necessitates an effect together. Thus, the soul exists together with its cause; this is because its cause possesses a perfect Essence and is complete in its advantage, and that which is so does not separate from its effect. Nevertheless, its influence in the body depends on a certain ability and specific conditions. And it is known that the soul comes into being on the body attaining complete preparedness and is subsistent with the body when it perfects."[48]

9- Soul In Its Unity Is All Of Its Faculties

Here also there are two opinions that have been narrated from the philosophers:

"Some were of the opinion that the soul is a single unit . . . It performs its acts all by itself, but through different means from each of which issues a specific action. This is the opinion of Ibn Sina and those of his level. Some others, however, hold that, 'Surely the soul is not one, but [made up of] numerous [parts], some of which are sensory, some intellectual, some sensual, and others wrathful."[49]

"And you shall soon come to know that for each of our bodies there is only one soul and that the rest of the faculties are its effects and offshoots in the parts of the bodies. This view was popular among the later authoritative theosophies. However, what we believe is that the soul is all its faculties, meaning that it is a unit that embraces all of the faculties and is their cause and end."[50]

"This refutation is of the matters I propounded for many of the contemporary scholars of my time, and none was able to solve its problem, until Allah enlightened my heart and guided me to the straight path . . . And that is that I beheld my soul and found it to be simple egoity (*inniyyah sirfah*)."[51]

10- Intermediate Immateriality Of The Faculty Of Imagination

Asfar writes:

"And although this matter is contrary to what the rest of the theosophers believe, including Shaykh and his ilk, that which is to be followed is intellectual proof. And the truth is not known save through intellectual proof. It is not known by looking at the personalities."[52]

"I did not find from the books of philosophers any research on this matter. Nor did I find any research on the notion of the immateriality of imagination, or on the difference between its abstraction from this material world and the abstraction of the intellect . . . the knowledge of this is from the things that Allah favored me with and guided me towards. I extremely thank Him and praise Him for this great blessing."[53]

From there, Asfar deduced the issue of the immateriality of the animal soul. He writes:

"Surely Allah inspired us by His Grace and Beneficence an Oriental proof on the immateriality of the animal soul that possesses the faculty of imagination from this world and its accidental properties."[54]

Moreover, Asfar interprets *"ajab al-dhanb,"* which refers to the remaining elements of the body after death, as the faculty of imagination.

"And the scholars differ in its meaning. It has been said that it stands for the material intellect (*al-'aql al-hayulani*). Others believe that it rather is 'matter' itself. Abu Hamid al-Ghazali says: 'Surely it is the soul, and the higher realm of the Hereafter originates upon its basis. And Abu Yazid Waqwaqi holds that it is a remnant substance of this world which does not change'. Shaykh al-'Arabi in his Futuhat says that it is a substantive reality (*'ayn al-thabit*) belonging to humans. The theologians believe that 'they are essential parts of the human being.' We, however, believe that it is the faculty of imagination, for it is the last entity acquired in man from material faculties."[55]

11- Invalidity Of Reincarnation

All Islamic metaphysicians and theologians reject the idea of 'reincarnation' as indicating 'a transfer of the spirit from the body it resides in to another body and its control over the latter. They have given several reasons why reincarnation should be considered invalid. Mulla Sadra did not find their arguments to be complete and perfect, and therefore presented another proof based on his discovery of the trans-substantial motion.

"The reason for Invalidity of reincarnation (*tanasukh*) is that the soul is essentially connected to the body and both are harmoniously and naturally united together and the fact that each of the two together with the other possesses an essential trans-substantial motion."[56]

"Hence the path to disprove the evil of reincarnation (*tanasukh*) is that which we mentioned before and singly expounded, and whose elucidation Allah made our share of the transcendent theosophy and religious knowledge, as He did so with relation to other such examples, that Allah inspired us with by the Grace of His Effusion and Beneficence."[57]

12- Possibility Of The Inferior

Of the well-known philosophical principles introduced by Aristotle is the principle of the possibility of the superior (*qa'idat al-imkan al-ashraf*). According to this principle, any entity cannot descend to a lower plane of existence unless it has crossed the higher planes. Mulla Sadra introduced a similar principle that refines this one: the 'principle of the possibility of the inferior' (*qa'idat al-imkan al-akhass*). According to this principle, existence cannot attain a more sacred level of contingent existence in the arc of ascent unless it has passed through all the lower levels in this arc.

13- Bodily Resurrection

The belief in resurrection is a doctrinal principle accepted by all the Divine religions and is among the roots of the Islamic religion. That which is inferred from the apparent contents of the Book of God and traditions of the Holy Prophet and his infallible progeny indicates that resurrection transpires both spiritually as well as materially.

The theologians were unable to prove the material dimension of this principle, and simply relied on what the Divine Revelation had brought. Avicenna says:

"It is imperative to know that from among the kinds of Return (Ma'ad) there is that which has been presented by the religion, and which we have no way of proving save through accepting the religion and adopting the tradition of the Prophet (A). And that is the Return of the body at Resurrection (ba'th)".[58]

However Mulla Sadra claims that he was able to prove the Bodily Resurrection and considers that to be one of the most distinctive features of his transcendent theosophy. And very few of the outstanding divine theosophers have researched on the knowledge of the Bodily Return (*al-Ma'ad al-jismani*) from the intellectual dimension.

"And our belief—that corresponds to the reality—concerning the Resurrection of the bodies on the day of Retribution is that the bodies shall be raised from their graves in such a way that if you were to see any one of them, you would be able to distinguish him and say 'this person is so and so.' They would not take the form of the people's *muthul* and *ashbah*. The verses of the Book and various faiths and religions tell us that what returns at the time of the Return is the soul together with body, and not just the soul. And it is not necessary for every human being to be raised with a body from the bodies. Rather, those who are perfect in the knowledge of Divine matters are only raised in front of Allah while they are totally separated from their bodies".[59]

Since matters pertaining to the Hereafter are beyond the realm of this world, the intellect cannot comprehend their realities.

"Beware lest you try to understand these matters by means other than traditions and belief in the Hidden, for if you try to understand them by means of your defective intellect and spurious guide you would resemble a blind man who wants to perceive colors by means of his sense of taste, smell, hearing, or touching. And this is a literal denial and refusal of the existence of color. Likewise, the covetousness to understand the states of the Hereafter through the process of reasoning and theology meets a literal denial and refusal thereof . . . ."[60]

14- *Transformation of the Human Being into Different Realities Depending on His Inner Self*

This discussion follows his statement on the fact that the Human spirit is materially contingent (*jismaniyyat al-huduth*) and spiritually subsistent (*ruhaniyyat al-baa*).

"Surely, the human soul is the final and best material form, the first spiritual entity and the lowest of them, for the reason that it is materially contingent, as well as spiritually subsistent. And surely, it comes into being through the potential in the body, while its essence continues changing by means of firmly fixed spiritual habits, from potentiality into actuality . . . And as Allah created different species (*anw'a`*) of animals in this world—among them domestic and predatory animals such as wild beasts, snakes and scorpions—he created different species of man from the spiritual matter in the Hereafter . . . The human being is one such species in this world . . . And very soon it will transform into many species that will have numerous and different genuses. And there are numerous verses in the Holy Qur'an that manifest what we have mentioned here, serving as our intellectual proof—and this is of what Allah has specifically inspired me from among the people of authority. And I have not found the same in anyone else's speech, from the Divine sages or others."[61]

"And this is the opinion that human souls in their primal genesis are from one species, but in their second makeup they transform into many species and their [respective] genuses. Although this view was not even one of the metaphysicians, it was what Allah had inspired us and lead us towards the proof of."[62]

15- Perception

Mullā Sadrā defines knowledge as Existence and regards it as a degree of Existence. Sadrā views the four kinds of perception (sensation, imagination, prehension and intellection) together with their different stages as one entity, which he sees as possessing certain strengths and weaknesses. Moreover, in the same way that Existence and essence are united, knowledge is conjoined with the known. For Sadra, in fact, knowledge is equivalent to the known. On the knowledge of possibilities and the knowledge of Man, he believed that there exists a union between the intellect and the intelligible. He regarded all perception as an effect of the unification between perceiver and perceived, and he viewed intellection and knowledge by means of the unifications between intellect, the intelligent and the intelligible, and between knowledge, knower, and the known, respectively.

Drawing on Sadra's philosophy, one can discuss the question of perception or knowledge from two fundamental dimensions: epistemological and ontological.

Mullā Sadrā has analysed the concepts of perception and/or knowledge from many perspectives in different places of his *"Asfār"*. In the chapters concerning ontology, he has examined whether Existence is objective or subjective and has defined one aspect of knowledge as being that of mental existence. In *"The Ten Categories"*, he considers whether or not knowledge is a mental quality and whether, moreover, the soul has the power to attain to knowledge. These questions are raised throughout the chapters *"Union between the intelligent and the intelligible"* and *"The knower and the known"*. In the third volume of his *"Asfār"*, he puts forward an independent study with regards to knowledge and related matters.

According to Sadra, perception occurs when the faculty of intelligence merges with the essence of the intelligible. Once this union is established, perception is achieved. Sadra defines perception as the Existence and union of the perceiver and perceived.[63] In other words, this true union is equivalent to perception, and this is the same definition as knowledge.

Interestingly, this is the same definition Sadra gives for knowledge, making perception and knowledge equivalent in his philosophical writings. Sadra denotes four kinds of perception:

(i) Sensation
(ii) Imagination
(iii) Prehension
(iv) Intellection

Sensation:

Sensation is the perception of an existing thing in the material world that is directly present before the perceiver with all its distinctive characteristics.

Imagination:

Imagination is the perception of a sensible thing together with all its distinctive characteristics; it (the imagined) is attained in the presence of (the thing's) matter (external world) and can be recalled even when absent, i.e., the imagined need not be directly present before the perceiver.

Prehension:

Prehension is that which is perceived as intelligible within a particular rather than a universal sense

Intellection:

Intellection is the perception of general concepts, meanings and substances and the reception of forms devoid of material dimensions.[64]

There are three pre-requisites to attaining sense perception:

(i) Material presence in front of the perceiving apparatus
(ii) The inclusion of distinctive characteristics of the thing perceived
(iii) The particularisation of the perceived

Hence, the first condition does not exist with respect to imagination; moreover, the first two pre-requisites are not necessary as far as prehension is concerned. Sadra regards knowledge—as with Existence—as transcending and not needing definition.⁶⁵ On explaining knowledge, he states that knowledge means the presence of a thing *qua* that thing.⁶⁶ He generally criticized Ibn Sina's and Shaykh Ishraqi's views on knowledge, believing that knowledge is not a meaningless command—like that of the separation from matter—nor is it an affirmative command; rather, knowledge is an existing command pertaining to an actual entity rather than a potential entity. Even then, only pure entities are alluded to, i.e. entities which are by no means mixed or associated with non-existence.

Sadra regards knowledge and Existence as being in possession of degrees. In the same way that some creatures are weak and miserly while others are strong and loyal, knowledge, too, possesses numerous degrees, some of which are weak (for example, sensation) while others are trustworthy, such as the intellect. Sadra sees knowledge as a method and a way of existence⁶⁷ in the sense that, similar to Existence, knowledge is in possession of different stages with respect to perfection and defection.⁶⁸ In *Kitab al-Māsha'ir*, Mullā Sadrā argues that "knowledge is nothing but presence of existence without any obstacles. Every comprehension is realized due to some mode of abstraction from matter and its obstacles. It is so because matter is the source of privation and absence; since each part of the body is absent from the other components, and absent from the totality, the totality becomes absent from the totality. Thus, the more intense is each form, in the sense of degree of purity from matter, the more sound is its presence to its inner-reality. The most base is the presence of the forms of the sensible to their inner-realities. Then, [flows] the forms of imaginable [entities] according to their different ranks. Subsequently, [we see] the forms of the intelligibles. The highest degree of intelligibles is the most forceful in existence—and that is The Necessary Existent".⁶⁹

Classification of Knowledge:

For Sadra, knowledge can be divided into two types: *knowledge by presence* and *acquired knowledge*. The groundwork of acquired knowledge is, in fact, based on knowledge by presence. Acquired knowledge may be further divided into representation and judgements, with representation being further divisible into universal and particular components. The latter components include modes of sensory, imaginary and prehension, whereas universal representational knowledge—which is labelled as 'intelligent concepts and intelligibles'—is used as the pivot for important philosophical discussions.

Universal concepts may be categorized into three types:

(i) Primary intelligibles, e.g., Man, whiteness
(ii) Secondary philosophical intelligibles, e.g. the rule of cause and effect
(iii) Secondary logical intelligibles, e.g. the principle of non-contradiction

Primary intelligibles occur and are subject to qualification in the external world, whereas secondary philosophical intelligibles occur in the mind but are qualified in the outside world only. Concerning the secondary logical intelligibles, both their occurrence and their qualification are essentially mental in origin.

Sadra believes in the union between the intellect, the intelligent and the intelligible, and also in the union between knowledge, the knower and the known.

16- Causation

Causation in Sadrian philosophy is a complex issue that operates on many levels. This section will introduce an ontological and epistemological approach to cause and causation, and will describe some of the divisions that have been proposed for a theory of causation. It concludes by considering some implications and consequences for understanding the relationship of causation to key Sadrian philosophical doctrines.

In Islamic Philosophy, the word "cause" is used in both a general and a specific sense. The general concept is applied to an existent upon which the realization of another existent depends, even if it is not sufficient for this realization. The specific concept is applied to an existent that is sufficient for the realization of another existent. The following two diagrams illustrate the Ontological and Epistemological approach on Causation in Mulla Sadra's Philosophy.

Mulla Sadra clarifies this distinction in *Asfar* and *Shawahed*, where he explores two senses of the word cause. The first sense describes a weaker relationship, and refers to a situation where a thing's existence or non-existence simply *obtains* from the existence or non-existence of another entity. The second, stronger type of causality refers to a relationship of direct reliance between entities. For Mulla Sadra, this second sense speaks to a situation where the existence of one thing relies on the existence of another;

so its non-existence makes it impossible but its existence does not make it necessary.[70]

According to Mulla Sadra, Being (*Wujud*) can be divided into cause and effect.[71] But the cause and effect are not examples of quiddity *(māhowi)* nor of primary intellect because their characterization (*ittisaf*) is external. Hence, these concepts are philosophically secondary.

Muslim theologians and philosophers have discussed the subject of the principle of causality. In considering the criterion of the need for a cause, Muslim theologians have thought the "emergence" ("*hudūth*") (coming into existence after being non-existent) is the subject. Contrary to this view, philosophers before Mulla Sadra believed that the subject of causality is contingency (*imkān*). According to this pre-Sadrian view, every existent which essentially has the possibility of non-being, such that the supposition of its non-being is not impossible, is in need of a cause.[72] For these scholars it followed that it is not intellectually impossible for an existent which is an effect to be eternal.

However, it is to be noted that the contingency (*imkān*) is the attribute of *(māhiyyah)* a quiddity. For this reason, the criterion for the need for a cause is regarded as an "essential-contingency" (*Imkān dhatī*).[73] But Mulla Sadra criticizes this view, in *Ibn-e Sina* and *Sohrevardi*, because essential-contingency is homogenous with the "fundamentality of quiddity" (*asalāt al-māhiyyah*). However, Mulla Sadra, who establishes the "fundamentality of existence" (*asālat al-wujūd*), has based his philosophical discussion on Existence. He says that the basis of the need of an effect for a cause is the mode of its existence. With attention to the levels of gradation of existence, in which each weaker level is dependent on a stronger level, the subject of the proposition can be considered "the weak existence" whose dependence on the need for a cause is due to the weakness of the level of existence. So, according to Mulla Sadra, the subject of the principle of causality will be "impoverished existent" (*mawjūd-e faqir*) or 'dependent existent'.[74] Hence, according to fundamentality of existence, firstly, the causal relation is to be sought in either the existence of the cause or the existence of the effect rather than in their whatness/quiddity *(māhiyyah)*.

Secondly, being an effect and the dependency of an effect are essential to its existence, such that the dependent existence will never be independent and without need of a cause.

On this basis, objective existence (*Wujūd-i 'einī*) divides into two parts, the independent and the relational (*mustaqil and rābit*).[75]

Every effect in relation to its creating cause is relational and dependent. Every cause in relation to the effect it creates is independent, however much it may itself be the effect of another existent, and in relation to that, it will be relational and dependent. The absolutely independent is a cause, which is not the effect of the existence of anything. This is one of the most valuable results of the Mulla Sadra philosophy.

Primary Cause or Absolute Cause:

On the basis of three principles of Mulla Sadra philosophy, i.e. "the fundamentality of existence", "the relativity of the effect in relation to the creative cause" and the "graduation of the planes of existence", it follows that every effect occupies a weaker position than its creative cause, and that its cause, in turn, occupies a weaker position than a more perfect existent which is its creative cause. This relay continues until we reach an existent that has no weakness, failure, deficiency or limitations. Such a final existent is infinitely perfect, and is no longer the effect of any other thing. The distinguishing feature of the absolute cause or cause of causes is the infinite intensity and perfection of existence.

The Reality of the Causal Relation:

According to Mulla Sadra the effect takes the form of a ray radiated by the existence of the cause, and incorporates both the relation itself and its very condition of dependence. The concept of relation is abstracted from its essence, and in technical terms it is said that the existence of the effect is an "illuminative relation" (*idāfah ishraqiyyah*) of the existence of the cause. As such it is not a relation to be considered as belonging to one of the categories abstracted by recurring relations between two things, such as ventured by Hume and his followers.

The divisions of causes are rational (*'aqli*) and yield mutually exclusive pairs of positive and negative terms. A cause understood in its general sense, that is, an existent upon which another existent is somehow dependent, may be classified in various ways, of which the following are the most important:

Complete and incomplete causes: A cause may take one of two forms. It may be sufficient for the realization of the effect, so that the existence of its effect depends on nothing other than it. Or a cause may be insufficient for the realisation of the effect, even though that effect cannot be realised without it. The former sort of cause is called a "complete cause" and the latter is called an "incomplete cause".[76]

Simple and compound causes: Simple causes include completely immaterial things. A simple cause is one that has no parts, and a composite cause is its opposite. A simple cause is either simple with regard to external reality, or it is simple from the viewpoint of the intellect. The simplest of entities, which is composed of existence and quiddity, is the Necessary Being, exalted in His Name. Compound causes include material causes composed of different parts.[77]

Proximate and remote causes of immediate and mediate causes: A proximate cause is one where there is no mediation between cause and effect, while a remote cause is one where there is mediation between cause and effect.

Internal and external causes: Internal causes correspond with matter and form, whereby the effect is constituted and sustained. External causes are the "agents" (i.e. efficient cause) and the "end" (i.e. the final cause). If the effect unites with its cause and the cause remains internal to the existence of the effect, it is called an interior cause while an external cause remains external to the existence of its effect.

Real and preparatory causes: Sometimes the concept of cause is applied to that existent upon which the existence of an effect is really dependent, so that it becomes impossible to separate it from the effect. These are called real causes. In the case of a "preparatory cause", or preliminary one (*al-muʻiddat*), the concept of cause is applied to that existent which prepares the way for the appearance of its effects, although the existence of the effect does not have a real and inseparable dependence on it.

The four Aristotelian causes (material, formal, efficient and final): The material cause is the ground for the appearance of the effect and remains intrinsic to it. The formal cause is the activity which appears in the matter and which becomes the source of the new effect in it. The efficient cause is the means by which the effect is brought about. The final cause is the motivation of an agent for the performance of the action.[78]

According to *Mulla Hadi Sabzewari* and *M.H. Tabātabāʼeī* Agents can be divided into eight types: "natural agents" (*faʻil bi l-tabʻ*), "constrained agents" (*faʻil bi l-qasr*), "intentional agents" (*faʻil bi l-qasd*), "compelling agents" (*fa'il bi l-jabr*), "subordinate agents" (*fa'il bi l-taskhir*), "providential agent" (*fa'il bi l-'inaya*), "agent by agreement" (*fa'il bi l-rida*)and "agent by self-disclosure"(*fa'il bi l-tajalli*).[79]

The Homogeneity (*Sinkhiyyat*) of Cause and Effect:

The homogeneity between the existence-giving cause and its effect means that this cause embodies the perfection of the effect in a more perfect form. If a cause in its own essence did not possess a kind of existential perfection, it would never be able to grant this perfection to its effect. In other words, every effect is produced by its cause, which has the perfection of its effect in a more perfect form. This subject becomes clearer with regard to the relational nature of the effect and its existence-giving cause and the special gradation between them, which were established in transcendent philosophy. With regard to this topic a problem may be raised. The solution to this problem becomes possible by virtue of the fundamentality of existence, and on the basis of the "fundamentality of quiddity"/*whatness,* there would be no correct solution for it.[80]

Unity of an Effect for Unity of a Cause:

According to a well-known philosophical principle, from a single cause nothing can be produced but a single effect, since "the one produces nothing other than the one" (*Alwahed la yasdero 'anh elal wahed*).[81]

Discussion:

According to Mulla Sadra's philosophy, since the causal relation really holds between two existences, it is clear that the quiddity (*Mahyyat*) of something cannot be considered the cause of its existence, for quiddity (*Mahyyat*) in itself has no reality such that it could really be the cause of something. Likewise, a quiddity (*Mahyyat*) cannot be considered the cause of another quiddity (*Mahyyat*).

The Impossibility of Infinite Causal Regress (*Mahal boodan-e tasalsul-e 'illal*):

In this regard *Farabi* presents *"Burhan-e Asadd Akhsar"* ('the firmest and most concise proof'), a proof (*Burhan*) that covers all real causes. Mulla Sadra founded a new proof on this subject, on the basis of the principles of transcendent philosophy.[82] Mulla Sadra's proof is restricted to existence-giving causes and complete causes.

According to the fundamentality of existence and the relatedness of the existence of the effect to 'the existence-giving cause', every effect in relation to its creative cause is just that relation and dependence itself. It has no independence of its own. If a given cause is an effect in relation to a prior cause, it will have that same state (of dependence) to the prior cause. Thus, if a chain of causes and effects is assumed, such that each cause is the effect of another cause, it will be a chain of relations and dependencies. It is self-evident that dependent existence cannot occur without the occurrence of an independent existence upon which the former depends.

Thus, inevitably there must be an independent existence beyond this chain of relations dependencies in the light of which all of them occur. Therefore, this series cannot be considered to be without a beginning and without an absolutely independent member.

Conclusion:

According to Prof. S. H. Nasr Mulla Sadra accepts the Aristotelian doctrine of the four causes and affirms the commentaries upon it by Ibn-e Sina and other earlier Islamic philosophers, but he transforms their conclusions completely by considering the relation between cause and effect in light of the doctrine of the principality of *wujūd* (*asālat al-wujūd*). In doing so he considers and combines horizontal and vertical causes, and his discussion of this subject leads to some of his most exalted gnostic (*'irfānī*) expositions.[83]

According to this section, in an epistemological approach on causation, the most important Mulla Sadra doctrines in relation with causation are as follow: 1-the concept of Being[84], 2-fundementality of Existence[85], 3-the gradation of Existence[86], 4-independent and relational Being[87], 5-Poverty Being[88], 6-illuminative relation 7-The One produces nothing other than the One, 8-Identity or union of Being and necessity, 9-Logical necessity of the order of Being, 10-The impossibility of infinite regress[89], 11-homogeneity of cause and effect.[90]

3. Mulla Sadra's Viewpoints on Different Schools of Thought

Mulla Sadra criticised the most important schools of thought, including Greek philosophers such as Plato, Aristotle, and Porphyry of Tyre, as well as Farabi, Ibn Sina, Suhrewardi, Nasir al-Din Tussi, Mir Damad, and Ikhwan al-Safa among the Muslim philosophers. He also crtisicised theologians such as Ash'rites, Mu'tazlites, Ghazali, Fakhr al-Din Razi, and Gnostics such as Ibn Arabi, Sadr al-Din Qunawi, along with Literalist scholars.

A- The Ancient Metaphysician

Mulla Sadra was of the opinion that the ancient metaphysicians acquired their beliefs from the Prophets and the saints, and that the source of the differences seen in their opinions were the symbolic allusions contained in their statements, which acted to safeguard theosophy from those who were incapable of appreciating the realities.

"And these obedient servants (*fuqara'*) have attained conviction of the fact that the school of thought of those high-ranking mystics, who had attained the stations of the firmly rooted saints and who sought their lights from the lamp of the perfect prophets—is the school of thought of those people of truth and conviction." [91]

". . . by virtue of their adoption of the path of the Prophets, the ancient scholars hardly made any mistakes when it came to espousing the significant roots and fundamentals of faith. That which is popularly attributed to them—that they believed in the pre-eternity of the world, God's ignorance and lack of power over particular substances (*al-juz'iyyᵢt*), and the denial of Bodily Resurrection—is [sheer] allegation against them, and a great lie."[92]

". . . Then, it is very well known that the habit of the ancient theosophers, in assimilating the path of the Prophets, was to explain their beliefs by way of indications (*rumuz*) and metaphors due to a wisdom they perceived or a benefit they observed, so that they could be in harmony with the feeble intellects and be merciful to them; and also, in order to be wary of the misled transgressive souls and their misunderstandings . . ."[93]

"And in short: the ancient philosophers possess allusions and secrets; and most of those who came after them denied the literal import of their statements and allusions, either because of ignorance or the negligence of their station, or perhaps due to their intense love of ruling over the creation."[94]

The extent of Mulla Sadra's belief in the ancient philosophers is apparent in his discussion on the temporal genesis of the material world. He quotes different opinions from them at the beginning of his discussion, and then tries to synthesize and justify their statements. He then says:

"... I hereby address them and turn to their souls, saying: 'O men of wisdom, how eloquent is your demonstration! O guardians of gnosis, how clear is your exposition! Not a thing I heard from you was unworthy of my highest praise and honor. Indeed, you have described the world in a manner overwhelming and Divine, and acknowledged the blessings of Allah in an intellectual and sacred level. You intelligently demonstrated the order of the heavens and the earth, and exhibited the arrangement of the realities in a wise and genuine manner. May Allah bestow on you the best of rewards for all that. How excellent is the power of the intellect that penetrated you, kept you steadfast, safeguarded you, and protected you from mistakes and lapses; and that also removed from you calamities and imperfections, and sickness and maladies."[95]

Those of them whom he mentioned by name and whose views he quoted were Empedocles, Alexander of Aphrodisias, Anaxagoras, Aristotle, Plato, Pythagoras, Zeno, Porphyry and Socrates.

Since he had no books other than those written by Aristotle and Plato, he quoted their statements from the later scholars such as Avicenna and Fakhr al-Razi, and mainly from al-*Milal wa al-Nahl* of Shahristani, *al-Amad 'alal abad* of 'Amiri and *Ta'rikh al-hukama* of Shahrzuri.

B- *Greek philosophers*

1- Plato

Mulla Sadra considers Plato to be among the greatest of the ancient theosophers.[96] Platonic Ideas (*al-muthul*) became popular through him in Islamic Philosophy. Mulla Sadra, after expurgating the Ideas and repelling the refutations presented against it, remarks:

"And I do not think that anyone ... all along these lengthy epochs attained, through intellectual conviction, an understanding of what [Plato] meant, save one unknown and isolated destitute [reference to himself]."[97]

That is why he tries to correct those popular views of Plato that contradict his own opinions, and interprets them according to his own beliefs. An example of this pattern can be found in Mulla Sadra's explanation of the soul's pre-existing relationship to the body.

An explanation of Mulla Sadra's position on the soul's relationship to the body will present in the chapter on soul.

2- Aristotle

Mulla Sadra greeted Aristotle's philosophy with admiration and praise. He said:

"Most of the statements of this very high-ranking philosopher reveal the power of his spiritual intuition and the light of his inner being, and manifest his proximity to Allah and the fact that he ranked among the perfect saints. And perhaps his engagement in the matters of the world, and his control of the affairs of the creation, including the reformation of the people and the renovation of the city, followed those austerities and inner struggles, and transpired after he had [already] gained control over his self and attained perfection in his essence. In that state, he became one who could not be distracted. He wanted to engage in both kinds of dominion and perfection in both the worlds. Hence he occupied himself in teaching and purifying the creatures and leading them to the path of guidance, for the sake of attaining proximity to the Lord of the creatures."[98]

Nevertheless, Mulla Sadra's final judgment about Aristotle is confronted with a difficulty from the ancient scholars. And that is the attribution of *Theologia* to him and the clear contradiction between what is contained in that book and what is contained in his other writings. Mulla Sadra has tried, at times, to harmonise these contradictions:

". . . that incapacitated the intellectuals who came after him to comprehend these luminary ideas (*al-muthul al-nuriyyah*) in its exact reality and affirm its existence, save for the First Teacher. Perhaps he supported it (luminary ideas) in some of his books and negated the same in most of his works. And it is as if he deemed it advisable to negate it."[99]

"Surely . . . it has been proven and become clear from the statements of this high-ranking philosopher . . . that he believed in the contingency of this world and its perdition . . . Hence that which the scholars understand and which has become popularly known among them is that he believed in the pre-eternity of the world. Perhaps what he meant by this is the pre-eternity of all that is beyond the material realm and material entities."[100]

"And if you were to say: 'You have contradicted the First Teacher, since he opposed this belief,' I would respond saying that the truth is more worthy to be followed. Besides, comprehending opposition from his side may have been a result of the (incorrect) understanding of the scholars who (merely) beheld the literal statements of Plato and the ancient theosophers. These thinkers were accustomed to communicating in the form of symbolic allusions and figurative expressions, especially in this type of discussion, where the eloquent can become tongue-tied and minds can become weary. . . . Alternatively, scholars may be reacting to the taint of [Aristotle's] love for ruling over creation according to the Divine laws that necessitates socialization with the creation and mixing with kings and rulers. Otherwise his book popularly known as "Theology" is a witness to the fact that his belief corresponds to the school of thought of his teacher in the section of the existence of intellectual forms of species and immaterial archetypes (*al-suwar al-mujarradah al-nuriyyah*)."[101]

Mulla Sadra's philosophy is against some of the most important doctrines of Aristotle's philosophy, such as: Necessity Being, God's knowledge, createdness or eternity of the world, existence, perception, substantial motion, intellect, creation, and soul-body relation. [102]

3- Porphyry

Porphyry made famous the notion of the unity of the intelligent and the intelligible and the unity of the soul with the active intellect. Mulla Sadra lauds him and considers him one of the most accomplished students of Aristotle.

"One of the high-ranking Divine theosophers who was firmly rooted in knowledge and Divine Unity is Porphyry, a companion of the Peripatetics and the author of Isagogic. To me he is one of the most high-ranking companions of the First Teacher, the most learned of the scholars in terms of the kernels of his ideas, and the most guided in his allusions and opinions on . . . the spirit and the Lord. He is also the most learned theosopher to address the nature of Resurrection and the return of the soul to the realm of the Truth and the abode of blessings."[103]

C- *Muslim Philosophers*

1- Farabi

Mulla Sadra calls Farabi "The Second Teacher" in recognition of his strong reputation as a follower of Aristotle and a Peripatetic philosopher. Sadra praises Farabi highly and often cites his statements as evidence. But on occasion Sadra does refute and reject Farabi's ideas.[104]

"As for the last opinion that al-Shaykh Abu Nasr held in synthesizing the two opinions and what Shaykh al-Maqtul preferred in the *"Hikmat al-Ishraq"*, then indeed we have invalidated it, as it was mentioned before."[105]

2- Ibn Sina

Mulla Sadra refers to Ibn Sina as, "The Shaykh of Islamic Philosophers" and "The eminent among the philosophers". Sadra frequently refers to Ibn Sina's works and propounds his opinions in all discussions. This tendency is manifested in his comprehensive gloss on the section on Divine matters (*ilahiyyat*) of his book *"al-Shifa"*. This gloss is known to rank among the best works of Mulla Sadra.

Ibn Sina also had a profound and undeniable effect on the construction of the transcendent theosophy. Prior to Mulla Sadra and Shaykh al-Ishraq, Sina struggled to prove mystical issues by means of rational demonstration, especially in the last two sections of his book *al-Isharat*. His efforts helped to simplify this difficult path for the theosophers who were to come after him.

In spite of his high praise for Ibn Sina, Mulla Sadra opposes him at various significant points and finds Sina unable to attain the truth of the matter. In his book Asfar he says that:

"And it is surprising to know that whenever his discussion reaches the point of proving the existential ipseities (*al-huwiyyat al-wujudiyyah*) before discussing Universal matters and all-embracing rules, his intellect gets clouded and he expresses his inability. And this is true in many instances."[106]

It is clear that Mulla Sadra was certain of Shaykh's ingenuity and radiant mind. Nevertheless Sadra expresses regret that this extreme astuteness is spent on matters that distract him from the primary search for Divine knowledge.

"It is not right for a theologian who is concerned with these matters to discuss at length on the *Isagogue* (Five universals) . . . and then, when he reaches the exalted matters and the realities of the secrets and the lights that represent the ultimate objective and firmest support, he shortens his discussion and leaves [off without] explaining many important issues, while also making mistakes in some of the subjects and Chapters . . ."[107]

3- The Master of Illumination, Shahab al-Din Suhrawardi

Shahāb ad-Dīn" Yahya Suhrawardī was a Iranian, philosopher, a Sufi and founder of the Illuminationist philosophy or "Oriental Theosophy", an important school in Islamic philosophy and mysticism. He is sometimes given the honorific title *Shaikh al-Ishraq* or "Master of Illumination" and sometimes is called *Shaykh al-Maqtul*, the "Murdered Sheikh", referring to his execution for heresy.

It was not possible to move from Peripatetic philosophy to transcendent theosophy without the appearance of illuminationist philosophy. And, Shaykh al-Ishraq, in introducing spiritual vision and disclosure into philosophy—and ceasing the method of pure rational demonstration—established a bridge that enabled Mulla Sadra to cross over and establish his specific philosophy, and the amalgamation of gnosis and philosophy.

Suhrawardi, in the introduction to his book, "*Hikmat al-Ishraq,*" after stating the method he has adopted in the rest of his works, says:

"And this is another course and a nearer method than that; it is more orderly, precise, and entails less difficulty in understanding; and I did not attain it at the onset through intellection. Rather, it first was attained in another way, and then I sought for its proof; so that if I was to overlook its proof, no skeptic would make me dubious about it . . ."[108]

He also says:

"And if the astronomical observations of one or two people are relied upon on issues pertaining to the heavenly bodies, how can the findings of the masters of theosophy and prophethood—on something they witnessed in their spiritual paths—not be relied upon?"[109]

And you find Mulla Sadra starts arguing by using his statement and adding to it the comments of the commentator of the Shaykh's book, Qutb al-Din Shirazi. He says in Asfar:

"And if they accepted the states of the stars and the numbers of the heavenly bodies according to the way of Epicures (*abarkhas*) or of others together with him through sense perception, which is vulnerable to falsity and disbelief, one would think they would consider—and, indeed, it would be more appropriate to do so—the findings of the masters of theosophy that depend on rigorous intellectual methods that allow for no mistakes."[110]

Furthermore, he ventured in this field to a more extensive and distant scope, and criticized the path of those who claim to comprehend matters pertaining to elevated knowledge (*al-'ilmu'l 'a'ala*) through mere discourse and intellection without seeking any help from spiritual vision (*kashf*). Indeed, he depreciated their approach and intensely reproached them, some of them which we have already mentioned.

Ishraqi's influence on Sadra is not limited to this particular matter. Rather, there is a semblance between many of their fundamental notions, as Sadra's transcendent theosophy itself is based on important aspects of the former. And this is why we find him revering the Shaykh as, '*the Possessor of an elevated spirit and very experienced in rational demonstrations*' and '*the Grand Shaykh.*'[111] He does not pass up the opportunity to venerate him, even when he observes something extremely baseless in his work:

"And this response is extremely ridiculous; and its issuance from a wise philosopher is extremely astonishing."[112]

Likewise, the extent of his attention to Illuminationist Philosophy is apparent from his comprehensive glosses on the "*Hikmat al-Ishraq*," which is filled with research and criticisms. It is considered to be one of the excellent writings of Mulla Sadra.

4- Khwaja Nasir al-Din Tusi

Tusi was known by a number of different names during his lifetime such as Muhaqqiq-i Tusi, Khwaja-yi Tusi and Khwaja Nasir. According to Mulla Sadra, Muhaqqiq Tusi is among the greatest Islamic philosophers, both in rank and intellect. He calls him, 'the most distinguished of the posterior scholars,' 'the proof of the Islamic theosophers,' 'the Lord of the researchers, the Bearer of the throne of theosophy and realization, Nasir al-Din Tusi, may his most holy spirit be sanctified.'[113]

His veneration for Tusi is attributed to the latter's efforts in approximating peripatetic and Illuminationist philosophy, and eventually for his struggle to construct the transcendent theosophy. It is also due to his steadfast confrontation against the attacks of the theologians such as Fakhr Razi,

Ghazali and Shahristani; his refutation of their oppositions; and his response to the doubts they had created.

Muhaqqiq Tusi, in writing his *"Tajrid al-'I'tiqad,"* presented speculative theology (*'ilm al-kalam*) in a correct and philosophical style, and expurgated it from futile elaborate discussions and senseless jabber, the collection and presentation of which some theologians preceding him laid importance on. Besides, we are not aware of anyone among the scholars who succeeds him in his combination of ministerial duties within an oppressive and sinful government, carrying out in-depth research on intellectual issues, and being extensively aware of narrative, as well as natural and mathematical disciplines.

5- Mir Damad

Mir Burhan al-Din Muhammad Baqir Damad, whose poetic *nom de plume* was *'Ishraq'* and who was also referred to as 'the Third Master' (after Aristotle and Farabi) is one of the most important tutors of Mulla Sadra. He derived the greatest benefit from him in his education of the intellectual sciences, which is why Sadra bestows such great honor on him in many areas of his works:

"My master, supporter and tutor in the fundamentals of religion and Divine matters, and the gnosis of realities and the principles of certainty, the most grand and luminous Seyyed. The most pure and holy Seyyed, the Divine theosopher and jurist, the master of his age, and the chosen one of his time; the great commander, the illuminative moon, the most learned of his age, the marvel of the time, known as Muhammad—and nicknamed as Baqar al-Damad al-Husayni—may Allah sanctify his intellect with Divine light..."[114]

Mulla Sadra learned most of the intellectual issues from this great teacher and was influenced by his distinct opinions. However, he also contradicted a number of his teacher's views and opposed him with regards to the extremely vital issue of the principality of existence, which became the basis of the transcendent theosophy and its foundational stone. Nonetheless, evidence of his coming under the influence of his tutor is apparent from a number of issues.

Mir Damad laid importance on solving the issue of the temporal created-ness of the world and presented, in this context, the view of a temporal created-ness of the world, writing his well-known *"Al-Qabasat"* (The

Firebands) to prove just that. Sadr al-Muta'allihin, however, did not find the work to be correct, and hence took up the challenge of solving the difficulties that he had found with it, writing his own treatise on the temporal genesis of the world, which he was proud of and goes on to mention in many of his books. And surely, Mir Damad had already alluded to the path that Mulla Sadra had adopted in solving the problem.

"Indeed, temporal creation (*huduth*) and annihilation in the world of the extension of time cannot be feasible, except through an oscillatory entity, the nature of whose substance undergoes a continual process of renewal and annihilation, and a flow of continual becoming and extinction, without attributing the cessation and lapse to a cause outside its essence." [115]

And it seems that this praise and faith was mutual as indicated by a couplet that Mir Damad recited in praise of his distinguished student:

"Your prestige and post, O Sadra, is paid tribute to by the heavens,

Plato also pays tribute to your excellence and knowledge,

On the chair of research, none has emerged like you"![116]

6- The Brethren Of Purity[117]

The Ikhwan al-Safa (The Brethren of Purity) was written by brothers from the Isma'eli sect who lived in the fourth century A.H. (10th century CE), and consisted of a set of epistles that formed an encyclopedia of the disciplines of their time. In it the authors explained the path they adopted, their beliefs, and methods of attaining felicity in both the worlds.

The organisation of this mysterious society and the identities of its participants have never been clear. Their esoteric teachings and philosophy are expounded in an epistolary style in the *Encyclopedia of the Brethren of Purity* (*Rasa'il Ikhwan al-safa'*), a giant collection of 52 epistles that would significantly impact later encyclopaedias. A good deal of Muslim and Western scholarship has been spent on just pinning down the identities of the Brethren and the century in which they were active.

These epistles profoundly influenced later thinkers, including Sadra, who referred to them in his own writings.

Some of Sadra's statements indicate that he considered the authors of the epistles to be one person:

'And the author of Ikhwan al-Safa was of that opinion,'

(Mulla Sadra. *Tafsir*, 3/78)

'... and that which many scholars believed, amongst who was the author of the Ikhwan al-Safa'.

(Mulla Sadra, *Asfar*, vol8, p139)

Sadr's veneration of the authors of the *Ikhwan al-Safa* is revealed to the reader through his overt support for some of his/their ideas. However Sadra also opposes them in some places and refutes their opinions.

7- THE LATER PHILOSOPHERS

Sadr al-Mutallihin was aware of the opinions of the later philosophers and read their works painstakingly, with a focus on those who were near to his time, such as Jalal al-Din Dawwani (1426-1502), Seyyed Ghiyath al-Din Dashtaki, al-Khafri and others. But he was rarely influenced by them in a direct way. He sometimes quoted their ideas and refuted them, but rarely gave them his full support.

D- The Theologians

When the author speaks of the theologians, he mostly aims at the Ash'arites, the Mu'tazilites and other corrupt sects. He considers their opinions to be futile and refutes them:

"Surely they are the people of innovations (*bid'ah*) and deviation (*al-dalal*) and leaders of the ignorant and depraved folk. All their evils are aimed at the religious and God-wary society and their inflictions at the *'ulama*; and they are extremely antagonistic towards the believing Divine theosophers. This argumentative and antagonistic society who delve in intellectual matters while they are [even] oblivious of the sensibilities..."[118]

"And I wish they limited themselves with the religion of the old people and satisfied themselves with unconditional following (*taqlid*); and I wish they would not decline saying the phrase 'we do not know...'"[119]

"The habit of most of these theologians is to argue without insight or conviction, presenting baseless premises coupled with many mistakes and confusing, faulty reasoning. Their work is filled with opinions which mislead the masses, so that even astute people may begin to think that the roots of religion can rest on such frail statements."[120]

"It is surprising that people of their ilk are regarded as authoritative by the masses. We apologize for presenting some of their excesses in this book. For an intellectual does not waste his time in enumerating and refuting thoughtless statements." [121]

1- Ghazali

Ghazali was a bridge between the theologians and the gnostics. For this reason, whenever he tries to oppose the theosophers and presents frail opinions, Sadr al-Muta'llihin condemns him as:

"One who took upon himself to be inimical towards the men of truth by way of opposition and disputation and who portrayed himself as spiritual while merely citing quotations. [In this sense he is] similar to one who fights against heroic figures and confronts the manly folk by merely carrying weighty items and weapons of war. He says in his work which he named *"Tahafut al-Falasafah"* (the Incoherence of the Philosophers) . . ."[122]

But when Ghazali showed his inclination towards *'irfan* and gnosis, Sadra praised and lauded him.

"We only introduced the statements of this billowing sea who was called Imam and *Hujjat al-Islam* [the proof of Islam] by the people, so that it may soften the hearts of the wayfarers of the path of the men of conviction."[123]

"Furthermore, these findings and interpretations on the Qur'anic secrets and the treasures of the All-embracing Divine Mercy form a short allusion of the simple descriptions of *Hujjat al-Islam* and a brief summary of the sieved catches out of this magnanimous sea. They are a product for the salvation of souls and a cure of the spirits and a summary of the path of guidance and felicity. For he is a vast sea from whose oysters the pearls of Qur'ın are taken, and a blazing fire from whose torch the lights of eloquence are obtained; his brilliant mind is a rarity from where the alchemy of ultimate salvation is taken; his penetrating mind derives pearls of meanings from the seas of root words . . ."[124]

Mulla Sadra justifies the apparent contradiction in his different views of Ghazali by saying that:

"The attestable truth is that al-Ghaz₁li, in most of the religious principles and roots of faith, followed the theosophers. He has taken most of his beliefs from them, finding their views on the Chapter of the Origin and the Return (al-Mabda' wa al-Ma'ad) to be intellectually perfect, pure of the taints of obscurity and doubt, and . . . farther from contrariety and contradiction than the statements of others.

However, the denial, rejection, refutation and disapproval that appear in his books may have been based in part on a religious desire to protect the beliefs of the Muslims from dissipation and loss of what they heard from the theosophers without understanding and perspicacity. [He may have wanted to] repel the rejection of their meanings and to protect their religion, so that their feet did not waver as a result of hearing from deficient folk and pseudo-philosophers that '. . . acquiring theosophy makes one independent of the Islamic Law . . .' . [Alternatively, his rejections may be read] as dissimulation (*al-taqiyyah*) and as resulting from the fear of being rejected by the literalists (*zahiriyyin*) among the jurisprudents of his time. It is well-known that one of his contemporaries charged him with disbelief and wrote a treatise on his disbelief and deviation. [Ghazili's refutations may also be explicable as an early phase in his thinking], prior to his proficiency and perfection in gnosis. Early on, he thought that they [the theosophers] negated the Almighty's Power and Knowledge of particular entities and rejected the bodily resurrection. Later, after contemplating their statements and appreciating the fact that they believe in the three aforementioned ideas in a subtle sense . . . . he returned in repentance and held their opinions and beliefs."[125]

He did not consider Ghazali's belief in Shi'ism to be far-fetched, and he frequently referred to Ghazali's books. One example of this pattern finds Sadra invoking Ghazali's views on the evils of analogic reasoning:

"And al-Ghazali considered it [judicial reasoning by analogy] to be invalid and regarded it to be from the yardsticks of Satan, for he said, 'As for the measure of analogical reasoning, God forbid that it is held onto; and whosoever of my contemporaries reckon it to be a measure of knowledge, then I pray to Allah to save the religion from his evil, for he is an ignorant friend, who is more evil than an intellectual enemy. His statements end over here, and they give off the scent of Shi'ism."[126]

2- Fakhr al-Din al-Razi

Perhaps one who views the books of Mulla Sadra would think that there is a contradiction between his reliance on the books of the Leader of the *mushakkikin* (Skeptics) and the numerous quotations from him in most of his works, not excepting his *"al-Mabahith al-Mashriqiyyah"* and his criticism and defamation of his opinions and condemnation of his writings.

"Surely whatsoever this distinguished personality, famous for leadership and knowledge amongst the laity, has alluded to does not pertain to the Holy Quran at all. Nor has he become, by cognizance of it, one of the upholders of the Holy Qur'an and among those exclusively well versed with it, as it has been narrated that 'The people of Qur'an are people of God and His chosen ones'. Rather all he has mentioned and alluded to of the many matters that have filled his books pertaining to speculative theology and jurisprudence, are either what has been heard from men or sheer imitation. [This is true of] most matters pertaining to Resurrection, and some issues concerning the Origin. His theological opinions and unstable principles cannot be relied upon to attain conviction and faith. Rather, it is only what a braggart would armor himself with [for use] in controversies and arguments . . . In short, none of these copious issues with which he brags is from the sciences of the Quran and that which concerns the men of God."[127]

Mulla Sadra looks at Razi from two angles, alternately praising and condemning him. He finds him to possess perspicacity, distinction and diligence in discussing and searching for opinions and beliefs, and notes his excellent disposition in portraying and narrating them. Hence he praises him and quotes the opinions from his books. On the other hand, Sadra faults him for rashness and hastiness, noting his tendency to contradict others without careful contemplation. Charging him with a lack of insight and an unwillingness to follow the leaders of truth, Mulla Sadra finally condemns and defames him:

"This man who is well known for distinction and perspicacity hastily opposes a personality like Ibn Sina prior to contemplation and research, due to his hasty disposition and rashness."[128]

"Far from imperfection is Allah. Has anyone like him been found in this world who has attained his level in excessive discussion and research and authoring several works and engaging in contemplation and then getting distant from the truth in such a manner, and becoming veiled from it in this way?"[129]

Razi's contribution and influence in the advancement of philosophy and speculative theology is beyond doubt. He excelled at raising numerous doubts and questions about every issue and performed a service by compelling thinkers to respond to and refute his arguments. However his influence is ultimately limited by an absence of penetrating views or correct opinions.

E- The Gnostics

Sadr al-Muta'llihin considered the Mystics (*'Urafa'*) to be the true theosophers, the people of truth and possessors of insight. For he was of the opinion that:

"Certainly the edifice of their views and the foundation of their opinions are based on radiant inspirations and sacred beams that are neither overcome by any taint of doubt and skepticism, nor any stain of deficiency and imperfection. They are not based on mere opinions of intellectual proof so that the doubts may quickly play with those who are fond of and depend upon them."[130]

Mulla Sadra's genius was in presenting intellectual proof of beliefs attained through spiritual disclosure and mystical findings.

The difference between him and them is:

"Surely among the habits of the Sufis is to suffice themselves with sheer spiritual vision and conscience in their beliefs. We, however, do not completely rely on that which has no convincing proof, nor do we mention it in our theosophical works."[131]

For example, "It became clear to them through a kind of conscientious apprehension and by searching through the lights of the Book and the Sunnah that everything possesses life and speech, and that everything remembers Allah, sanctifies Him, and prostrates for Him . . . And we knew that by the Grace of Allah, through intellectual reasoning and spiritual apprehension. And this is a quality with which, by the Grace and support of Allah, we are privileged."[132]

1- Muhyi al-Din bin al-'Arabi

Mulla Sadra rarely venerates anyone as completely as he does Ibn al-'Arabi. He believes him to be "The prototype of those who experience spiritual intuitions."[133] "We believe that he is among the men who experience spiritual disclosure."[134]

From what is apparent in his writings, Sadra also regarded him to be an Imamite (Shi'a). In his commentary to the *Usul al-Kafi*, after quoting statements of Ibn al-'Arabi on the Awaited Imam ('a), he says:

"Know first of all that most of what we quoted of his statements are present in the texts of tradition: some have been narrated by traditionalists from our bent, while others [have been told] through other chains of narrators. Then behold, O brothers, the ideas—hidden in the midst of his statements—that reveal his belief! For example his statement: 'Indeed Allah has a vicegerent,' and: 'the people of Kufa would be most helpful to him,' and his statement: 'his enemies would be the followers of the people of *ijtihad* among the *'ulama*,' and: 'Surely this is out of deviation,' and his statement: 'Because they believe that the people of ijtihad and its age are terminated,'... until the end of his statement."[135]

He rarely contradicts Ibn 'Arabi or declines to justify his statements. In short, the influence of Ibn 'Arabi's thoughts on the primary issues of Mulla Sadra's philosophy is undeniably clear.

2- Sadr al-Din Qunawi

A student of Ibn al-'Arabi, Sadr al-Din Qunawi gathered all the dispersed statements of Ibn 'Arabi in his books, and transferred them into a didactic style. This helps to explain why Sadra was so inspired by his writings. The most vivid example of this is seen in his Commentary to the Chapter of *al-Fatiha*, where he quotes whole paragraphs from the book *'I'jaz al-Qur'an'* of Qunawi.

Sadra's inspiration by him and praise for him is mainly due to Qunawi's commentary of the statements of his teacher and the transcription thereof, as is also the case with the rest of his followers.

3- Other *'Urafa*

'Ayn al-Quzat Hamadani is another gnostic from whose books sadr al-Muta'llihin narrates. In his book *'Zubdat al-Hagha'iq'* he elucidates matters that concern spiritual intuition in the language of the people of intellectual demonstration. [what does this mean? Who are the people of intellectual demonstration?] That is why his name has been recorded in the history of the formation of the transcendent theosophy.

Among other gnostics are 'Alā' al-Dawla Simnani and Suhrawardi,-the author of 'Awarif al-Ma'rif, Khwja 'Abdullah Ansari, Jalal al-Din Rumi, 'Abd al-Razzaq Kashani and others.

F- *Al-Mutusawwifah*

Al-Mutusawwifah refers to those men who call the people towards the truth and consider themselves to possess the station of Directorship and the Spiritual Pole (*qutbiyyah*), but who actually deceive the lay men in the process. Because they do not demand any purification of the soul from their followers—due to the fact that they themselves lack the same—the lay men, who naturally and innately love to possess the gnosis of God, choose to follow them. However, it is difficult for them to engage in the religious austerities. Therefore these ignorant leaders remove this hurdle from their path, and subsequently, the people get inclined to them. And in this way they acquire wealth, status and fame in the city.

They became affluent and gained acceptance by the government because they safeguarded the interests of the rulers and authorities. This resulted in still greater fame and enabled them to remain at ease in the city:

"This group is oblivious of the remembrance of God; how [then] can they be of the people of the spiritual heart? If an atom's weight of gnosis would shine in their hearts, how would they consider the door of the oppressors and people of the world as their *qibla*?"[136]

And when he mentions their interpretations of religious texts, he says:

"And this is how the Esoterics (*Batiniyyah*) sought to vanquish the entire religion by interpreting its apparent imports and subjecting them to their personal opinions. Hence to [avoid] getting duped by their ruse is essential, for their evil influence on religion is worse than that of the Satans. This is because the Satans, through their help, defend themselves when fighting to remove religiousness from the hearts of the Muslims."[137]

K- The Literalists (*Al-'Ulama' al-Zhiriyyun*)

According to Mulla Sadra point of view the formalists must know their limitations, and they must know that "above every possessor of knowledge, there is a Knower." The esoterics must safeguard the exoteric form and abstain from unveiling secrets to those who cannot bear to understand them. Indeed, the Almighty, relating what the virtuous servant told Moses ('a), says: "Assuredly you will not be able to bear with me patiently. And how should you bear patiently that which you have never encompassed in your knowledge" (Holy Quran 18:67-68).

"Scholars are of three kinds: 'One kind knows Allah, but is ignorant of His Command . . . and one kind knows the command of Allah, but is ignorant of Allah (this kind of scholar knows that which is lawful and prohibited, and is aware of the intricacies of the Divine Law, but is ignorant of the secrets of Allah's Majesty); and then there is one who knows [both] Allah and His Command"[138]

We believe in all of the above; and we know that the formalists must not become attached to the world and its adornments, that they must not follow the rulers and authorities in their vain desires, and that they must not join the ranks of the evil scholars:

"The greatest of the calamities that prevent one from beholding the secrets of religion and from witnessing the lights of conviction . . . is the belief that the literalists and the worldly scholars, who yearn after evanescent and fleeting pleasures, are the guides of creation and the presidents of religion, and that the scholars of personal opinion in juridical matters seek the Hereafter and the Final Return. And this is the greatest sedition in religion and the greatest obstacle in the path of the believers, for these are the highway robbers of truth and certainty. And isn't this similar to considering a sick ignoramus to be an expert doctor, or reckoning a spendthrift robber to be trustworthy? 'They know the covert dimension of the world and are oblivious of the Hereafter' (30:7)"[139]

Bibliography:

Ibn Sina, 1363, *Al-Isharat*, Trans and commentary, Malik Shahi, Hassan, Tehran.
Akbarian, Reza, 2009, *The Fundamental Principles of Mulla Sadra's Transcendent Philosophy*, Philadelphia.

Akbarian, Reza, 2009, *Islamic Philosophy: Mulla Sadra and the quest of Being*, Philadelphia.
Amin, S.H, 1975, *The Philosophy of Mulla Sadra*, Albany.
Ashtiyani, Jalal al-Din, 1981, *Sharhi-I hal wa ara'-I falsafi-yi Mulla Sadra*, Tehran.
Bydarfa, Mohsen, 1363, *Introduction to Tafsir al-Quran* by Mulla Sadra, vol 1, ed. Khawjawi, Mohammad, Qum.
Daftari, Abdulaziz, 2011, *Mulla Sadra, and Mind-Body Problem*, London.
Dinani, Ibrahim, 1982, *General Philosophical Principles in Islamic Philosophy*. Tehran.
El-Bizri, Nader, 2008, *Epistles of the Brethren of Purity. Ikhwan al-Safa' and their Rasa'il* (1st ed.). Oxford.
Morewedge, Parviz, 1992, *The Metaphysics of Mulla Sadra (al-Masha'ir)*, New York.
Morris, James (ed.) and trans. 1981, *The Wisdom of the Throne*, Princeton.
Mulla Sadra, 1981, *Al-hikma al-muta'aliya fi l-Asfar al-'aqlliyya al-arba'a*, 3rd edn, Beirut.
---. *Al-Taliqat 'ala al-Shefa*, Entesharat Bidar, Qum.
---. *Al-Masha'ir*, Tehran.
---. 1967, *Al-Shawahid al-rububiyya*, ed. Ashtiyani, Seyed Jalal al-Din, Mashhad.
---. 1976, *Al-Mabda' wa l-Ma'ad*, ed. Ashttiyani, Seyed Jalal al-Din, Tehran.
---. *Asfar*, Entesharat Dar al-Maarif al-Islamiah, Qum.
---. 1341, *al-'Arshiyyah*, Esfahan.
---. 1360, *Asrar al-Ayat*, Tehran.
---. 1363, *Asrar al-Ayat*, trans. Khajawi, Mohammad, Tehran.
---. *Iksir al-'arefin*.
---. *Kasr asnam Jahelyat*, ed. and trans. Bydarfa, Mohsen, Qum.
---. 1363, *Mafatih al-Ghayb*, Tehran.
---. 1386, *Majmueh Ash'ar-e Mulla Sadra*, ed. Khajawi, Mohammad, Tehran.
---. 1377, *Resaleh Huduth al-'alam*, 2nd edn, Trans. and eds Khawjawi, Mohammad Tehran.
---. 1383, *Sharh-e Usul-e Kafi*, trans. Khajawi, Mohammad, Tehran.
---. 1376, *Sih Asl*, ed, Khajawi, Mohammad, Tehran.
---. 1377, *Tafsir Sureh Waqiah*, 2nd edn, trans. and descriptive remarks by Khawjawi, Mohammad, Entesharat Mulla, Tehran.
---. *Tafsir al-Quran al-Karim*, Vol 1, ed. Khawjawi, Mohammad, Entesharat Bidar, Qum.
---. *Waredat Qalbi dar M'arefat Rububi*, ed. and trans. Shafi'iha, Ahmad, Tehran.
Nasr, S.H, 1978, *Sadr al-Din Shirazi and his Transcendent Theosophy*, Tehran.

Nasr, S. H & Leaman, Oliver (eds) 1996, "Mulla Sadra: His Teachings," in *History of Islamic Philosophy*, London.
Qaysari, Dawud, *Rasail*, Tehran, Anjuman Hekmat.
Rahman, Fazlur, 1976, *The Philosophy of Mulla Sadra*, Albany.
Safavi, Seyed G (ed), 2002, *Perception According to Mulla Sadra*, Tehran.
---. 2002, *A Comparative Study On Islamic Philosophy and Western Philosophy*, Tehran.
---. 2003, *Mulla Sadra and Comparative Philosophy on Causation*, Tehran.
---. 2011, *Soul From the Perspective of Mulla Sadra's Philosophy*, London.
Sosa, E. and Toolley, M(eds), 1998, *Causation*, Oxford.
Suhrawardi, Shahab al-Din, 1977, *Musanefat*, Anjuman Falsafeh, Tehran.
---, 1954, *Hikmat al-ishraq*, Tehran.
Ziai, Hussein, 1996, "Mulla Sadra: His Life and Works," in *History of Islamic Philosophy*, eds Nasr & Leaman, London.

Endnotes:

[1]. See: "What is the Transcendent Philosophy?", in *The Fundamental Principles of Mulla Sadra's Transcendent Philosophy*, Akbaryan, Reza, pp. 41-83.
[2]. Ibn Sina, Glosses on *al-Shifa'*,p 256.
[3]. Mulla Sadra, *Asfar*, 5/320.
[4]. Ibn Sina, *al-Isharat*, Namat.10, fasl. 9, p.468.
[5]. Suhrawardi, Commentary on *al-Isharat*. 7, 3, 401.
[6]. Qaysary, *The Epistles of Qaysari*, p.15.
[7]. Mulla Sadra, *Tafsir sureh Waqiah*, tarjemeh wa tashih, Khawjawi.p. 9.
[8]. Mulla Sadra, *Tafsir sureh al-Baqarah* 3, 376.
[9]. Mulla Sadra, Rasail Mulla Sadra, *Sarayan al-Wujud*, p. 138.
[10]. Mulla Sadra, *Asfar*, 5/205.
[11]. Kulainy, *Sharh UsuL al-Kafi*, Introduction to Kitab al-Hujja, p. 438.
[12]. Mulla Sadra, *Asfar*, 8/303).
[13]. Mulla Sadra, *Mafatih al-Ghaib*, p. 41.
[14]. Mulla Sadra, *al-'Arshiyyah*, p. 285.
[15]. Mulla Sadra, *Asfar*, 7/326.
[16]. Mulla Sadra, Asfar, 6/263.
[17]. Kulainy, *Sharh Usul Kafi, hadith no.1, Bab al nawadir, Kitab Tawhid*.
[18]. Mulla Sadra, *Asfar*, 1/152.
[19]. Mulla Sadra, *Asfar*, 3/446.
[20]. Mulla Sadra, *Asfar*, 6/6.
[21]. See: Akbarian, Reza, 2009, *The Fundamental Principles of Mulla Sadra's Transcendent Philosophy*, Philadelphia.

22. See: Akbarian, Reza, 2009, *Islamic Philosophy: Mulla Sadra and the quest of Being*, Philadelphia.
23. Mulla Sadra, *Asfar*, 1/49.
24. Mulla Sadra, *Asfar*, 1/47.
25. Mulla Sadra, *Asfar*, vol.1, p.380.
26. Mulla Sadra, *Asfar*, vol.2, p. 292.
27. Mulla Sadra, *Asrar al-Ayat*, P 146.
28. Mulla Sadra, *Taliqat al Hikmat Ishraq*, p 239.
29. *Asfar*, vol 3, p 78.
30. Mulla Sadra, *Mafatih al-Gyaib*, p 364.
31. ibid, p 387.
32. Kulainy, *Sharh Usul al-Kafi, bab al-Kun wa al-Makan, Seventh hadith*, p. 243.
33. Mulla Sadra, *Asfar*, v 3, p 312.
34. Mulla Sadra, al-Mabda' wa al-Ma'ad, p 93.
35. See: Safavi, S. G., 2002, "God in Greek and Islamic Philosophy" in *A Comparative Study On Islamic Philosophy and Western Philosophy*, pp. 7-46.
36. Mulla Sadra, *Asfar*, v 4, p 280.
37. Mulla Sadra, *Asfar*, v 6, p284.
38. Mulla Sadra, al-Kafi, Section 11, commentary on First Hadith, *Bab Jawami' al Tahid*, p 337).
39. Mulla Sadra, *al-Shawahid al-Rububiyyah*, P 39.
40. Mulla Sadra, *Asfar*, v 2, p 49.
41. Mulla Sadra, *Asfar*, v 6, p 110.
42. Suhrawardi, *Collected works of Shaikh Ishraq*, v 2, p 156.
43. Mullsa Sadra, *Asfar*, v 1, p 307.
44. Mulla Sadra, *al-Arshiyyeh*, p 241.
45. Mulla Sadra, *Asfar*, v 3, p 507.
46. *Asfar*, v 2, p 62.
47. See: Safavi, Seyed G, 2011, Soul Frome the Perspective Mulla Sadra's Philosophy; "Philosophycal comparison between the perspective of Mulla Sadra and Descartes on Soul",Safavi, Seyed G. *Transcendent Philosophy*: An International Journal for Comparative Philosophy and Mysticism, Vol. 1, Number 11, (December 2010), pp. 5-20.; Daftari, Abdulaziz, 2011, *Mulla Sadra and Mind-Body Problem*.
48. Mulla Sadra, *Asfar*, v 8, p 346.
49. *Asfar*, v 7, p 57.
50. *Asfar*, v 8, p 51.
51. *Asfar*, v 7, p 255.
52. *Asfar*, v3, p475.
53. *Asfar*, v3, p 479.
54. Mulla Sadra, *Mafatih al-Ghayb*, p. 509.

55. *Mafatih al-Ghayb*, p. 605, *Asfar*, vol 9, p.221.
56. *Asfar*, vol 9, p.2.
57. Mulla Sadra, *al-Mabda' wa al-Ma'ad*, p379.
58. Ibn Sina, *al-Shifa*, al-ilahyyat, Article 9, section seven.
59. Mulla Sadra, *Tafsir sureh Sajdah*, p.73.
60. Mulla Sadra, *Tafsir Sureh Yasin*, p. 150.
61. Mulla Sadra, *Asrar al-Ayat*, p. 142.
62. *Asfar*, vol.9, p.20.
63. Mullā Sadrā, *Asfār*, vol. 8, 40.
64. Mullā Sadrā, *Asfār*, vol. 1, 324.
65. Mullā Sadrā, *Asfār*, vol. 3, 271.
66. Mullā Sadrā, *Asfār*, vol. 2, 237.
67. Mullā Sadrā, *Asfār*, vol. 1, 290.
68. Mullā Sadrā, *Asfār*, vol. 3, 378.
69. Mullā Sadrā, *Kitāb al-Mashā'ir*, English translation by Morewedge, 63.
70. Mulla Sadra, *Asfar* (Beirut, 1981), Vol.2, 121; *Shawahed al*-Rubuiya (Mashhad, 1967), 68.
71. Mulla Sadra, *Shawahid*, 68.
72. Mulla Sadra, *Asfar*, Vol.1, 403.
73. Mulla Sadra, *Asfar*, Vol. 2, 389.
74. Mulla Sadra, *Asfar*, Vol. 2, 202.
75. Muhammad Hussayn Tabatabaei, *Nihayat al-Hikmah* (Tehran, 1991), part 2.
76. Mulla Sadra, *Asfar*, Vol. 2, 127.
77. Tabatabaei, *Nihayat al-Hikmah*, part8, chap 2.
78. Mulla Sadra, *Asfar*, Vol. 2, 129; Vol. 5, 27; Vol. 6, 127.
79. Tabatabaei, *Nihayat al-Hikmah*, part 8, chap 7.
80. Mulla Sadra, *Asfar*, Vol. 7, 236.
81. Dinani, Ibrahim, General *Philosophical Principles in Islamic Philosophy* (Tehran, 1982), Vol. 2, 267.
82. Mulla Sadra, *Asfar*, Vol. 1,144-147; Vol. 2, 141-169.
83. S.H. Nasr and O. Leaman, *History of Islamic Philosophy* (Tehran, 1995), part I, 656.
84. Mulla Sadra, *Asfar*, Vol. 1, 35.
85. Mulla Sadra, *Asfar*, Vol. 1, 10.
86. Tabatabaei, *Nihayat al Hikmah*, part 1, chap 3.
87. Tabatabaei, *Nihayat al Hikmah*, part 2.
88. Mulla Sadra, *Asfar*, Vol. 2, 202.
89. Tabatabaei, *Nihayat al-Hikmat*, part 8, chap 5.
90. Mulla Sadra, *Asfar*, Vol. 7, 236.
91. Mulla Sadra, *Resaleh Huduth al-'alam*, p.186.
92. Mulla Sadra, *Asfar*, vol 6, p.5.

93. Mulla Sadra, *Asfar*, vol.8, p.364.
94. Mulla Sadra, *Asfar*, vol.1, p.211.
95. Mulla Sadra, *Resleh al-huduth al-'alam*, p.321-322.
96. See Mulla Sadra point of view on Platonic Spirt at: Khamenei, Seyyed Muhammad, *"Mulla Sadra's Philosophy of Platonic Spirit"*, **at: http://www.mullasadra.org/new_site/english/.**
97. Mulla Sadra, *Asfar*, vol3, p507.
98. Mulla Sadra, *Asfar*, vol9, p109.
99. Mulla Sadra, *Asfar*, vol5, p216.
100. Mulla Sadra, *Asfar, vol5, p23.)*
101. Mulla Sadra, *Asfar*, vol2, p64.
102. See: Nasr, Seyyed Hossein, "The Quran and Hadith as source and inspiration of Islamic philosophy", in *Historey of Islamic philosophy* (ed), Nasr and Leaman.
103. Mulla Sadra, *Asfar*, vol5, p242.
104. See: "Knowledge as the Unity of the Intellect and the Object of Intellection in Islamic Philosophy: A Historical Survey from Plato to Mulla Sadra", Ibrahim Kalin.*Transcendent Philosophy*: An International Journal for Comparative Philosophy and Mysticism, Vol. 1, Number 1, (June 2000), pp. 73-91.
105. Mulla Sadra, *Asfar*, vol9, p192.
106. Mulla Sadra, *Asfar*, vol9, p109.
107. Mulla Sadra, *Taliqat Shifa*: 176.
108. Suhrawardi, *Musanefat*, vol.2, p.10.
109. Suhrawardi, *Musanefat*, vol.2, p.156.
110. Mulla Sadra, *Asfar*, vol.1, p.307.
111. Mulla Sadra, *Asfar*, vol 5, p 98; vol 6, p 253.
112. Mulla Sadra, *Asfar*, vol.7, p.315.
113. Mulla Sadra, Asfar, vol2, 149; al-Mabda wa al-M'aad, p 240.
114. Mulla Sadra, *Sharh Usul min al-Kafi*, al-Hadith al-awal, p.16.
115. Mir Damad, *al-Qabasat*: 305.
116. Mir Dmad, *Divan*.
117. See: El-Bizri, Nader (2008). *Epistles of the Brethren of Purity. Ikhwan al-Safa' and their Rasa'il* (1st ed.). Oxford University Press.
118. Mulla Sadra, *Asfar*, vol1, p.363.
119. Mulla Sadra, *Asfar*, vol9, p.201.
120. Mulla Sadra, *Shawahid*, p.271.
121. Mulla Sadra, *Asfar*, vol1, p78.
122. Mulla Sadra, *Asfar*, vol1, p.227.
123. Mulla Sadra, *Asfar*, vol2, p.326.
124. Mulla Sadra, *Mafatih al-ghayb*, p. 97.
125. Mulla Sadra, *al-Mabda wa al-ma'ad*, p.403.

126. Mulla Sadra, *Sharh al-usul al-Kafi*: bab nahi an al-qul bighayr 'ilm, al-hadith al-tase:169.
127. Mlla Sadra, *Sharh al-usul min al-Kafi*, bab al-rad ila al-ketab wa al-Suna, al-Hadith al-awal, p.199.
128. Mulla Sadra, *T'aliqat al-Shifa*, p.238.
129. Mulla Sadra, *Asfar*, vol2, p. 207.
130. Mulla Sadra, *Asfar*, vol1, p.307.
131. Mulla Sadra, *Asfar*, vol9, p234.
132. Mulla Sadra, *Asfar*, vol7, p.153.
133. Mulla Sadra, *Asfar*, vol9, p.45.
134. Mulla Sadra, *Tafsir*, vol3, p.49.
135. Mulla Sadra, *Sharh usul al-kafi*, al-hadith 21 min ketab al-'aql wa al-jahl, p.111.
136. Mulla Sadra, *Sih Asl*, p.18.
137. Mulla Sadra, *Kasr Asnam al-jahilih*, p.30.
138. Mulla Sadra, *Tafsir Sureh Hadid, p.*214.
139. Mulla Sadra, *Tafsir Sureh Yasin,* 142.

God in Greek and Islamic Philosophy: A Comparative Study of Aristotle and Mulla Sadra Shirazi on the Necessary Existent

Introduction

The nature of God, or the demiurge-creator and designer of the cosmos, is a venerable subject in philosophy and natural theology. In the Abrahamic faiths, and especially within a philosophical context, most medieval religious discussion about God, including the ontological and cosmological proofs for His existence, stems from the famous proof of the Prime Unmoved Mover in Aristotle's *Physics*. It was this proof, alongside later, more ontological proofs, associated with Anselm and Avicenna, that underpinned medieval philosophical theology. For this reason it is instructive to trace the development of philosophical theology from Aristotle through to the more sophisticated arguments about God found in the later Islamic tradition. In tracing this development we can see the creative thought of the monotheists who discuss God within a broadly Aristotelian context, and with reference to Aristotelian axioms. The present paper begins with Aristotle's theology—his concept of God and His attributes—and then compares this architectonic, foundational theology to the later philosophical theology of Mulla Sadra, which represents a richer and more sophisticated concept of God, indicative of a mature and confident Islamic philosophical tradition.

God in Aristotelian Philosophy

Aristotelian philosophy is marked by the lack of an explicit discourse on, or clear concept of, God. This seems all the more unusual given that the medieval discourse on God relies upon an Aristotelian philosophical system. Commentators and scholars of the Aristotelian corpus differ widely regarding Aristotle's views on God, especially on the question of whether the terms the "Prime Mover" and the "Active Intellect" refer to the One God or not.[1] The issue is further complicated in monotheistic traditions which stress the exclusivity of the One God, since there seems to have been little sympathy in Aristotle's world for monotheism, as opposed to the widespread beliefs in polytheistic and henotheistic practices.[2] It was only in late antiquity that the Near East, which was within the sphere of Hellenising philosophy, began to adopt monotheism, a trend that actually prefigures the coming of Islam.[3]

This inquiry will begin with Aristotle's proof for the existence of the prime mover, which this author, like many others, does interpret as his proof for the existence of God.

We shall begin this inquiry by considering Aristotle's proofs for the existence of God, and then move on to consider the attributes and properties of the Aristotelian deity. The most well-known proof for the existence of God attributed to Aristotle is the proof of the "Prime Mover." In this proof, Aristotle begins with physics. The proof is based on five principles:

1. Motion *(kinesis, haraka)* requires a mover *(muharrik)*.
2. Both *mover* and motion are simultaneous, meaning that it is impossible to conceive of a temporal separation between the two.
3. Every *mover* is either in motion *(mutaharrik)* or stationary *(thabit)*.
4. Every physical entity is in change *(mutaghayyir)* and in motion *(mutaharrik)*.
5. Infinite regress *(tasalsul)* is impossible.

The conclusion drawn from these five principles is that the chain of entities in motion ends at a mover, which is not itself in motion.[4]

The First Proof: The Prime Mover

In Books VII and VIII of the *Physics*, Aristotle provides elaborate discussions of motion.[5] He discusses certain characteristics of motion, and then, employing these and other primary concepts, he proves the existence of a mover who is unmoved as mentioned above. He enumerates the following premises:

1. Every motion has a *mover*.
2. Both the *mover* and motion are necessarily simultaneous.
3. Motion is both pre-eternal and eternal.

Thereafter he says:

> "Since everything that is in motion must gain motion by means of an agent, let us take the case in which a thing is in motion, and is moved by an agent that is itself in motion; and that agent too gains its movement from another agent, which is likewise in motion; and this latter agent too gains its motion from another thing; and this continues up until a certain point. Obviously, this chain cannot have an infinite regress; rather, there must be a Prime Mover . . . For the movements must reach an end [given the impossibility of Infinite Regress]. [. . .] The prime mover that is unmoved is Eternal and One. Since motion must always exist without any pause, there must be a first agent of motion which is eternal and unmoved [. . .] Since motion is eternal, then the first agent of change (which is one) would also be eternal. (We should assume that there is one first agent rather than a plurality, and a finite number rather than infinitely many). [. . .] We do not need to assume that there are more than one and since it is eternal and the first unmoved agent of motion, it will be the source of motion for everything else".[6]

The Second Proof: The Priority of Actuality Over Potentiality, and the Latter's Dependence on the Former

This proof is extrapolated from Aristotle's discussion of potentiality (*dunamis*) and actuality (*energeia*). The temporal and logical precedence of actuality over potentiality can be employed to prove the existence of an essential entity, which is Sheer Actuality.

The proof is as follows: everything comes into existence from potentiality to actuality, and, for one reason or another, everything requires an entity other than itself to transfer it from potentiality to actuality. It requires a sufficient reason or a preponderator to bring it into being.[7] It is necessary that an entity that transfers something from potentiality to actuality must itself depend upon an entity that is actuality in all its dimensions, and that does not itself depend on another entity; otherwise, the result would be a vicious circle or infinite regress. The entity that is actuality in all its dimensions is the Necessary Existent, or the Mover that is not in motion: the "Prime Mover".[8]

The Third Proof: The Chain of Causes Cannot Regress Infinitely

In his *Metaphysics,* Aristotle says:

> But evidently there is a first principle, and the causes of entities are neither infinite as a series or in a perspective. For neither the derivation from matter nor relative terms can sustain an infinite regress; nor can the source of change. Similarly, final causes cannot sustain an infinite regress. And the case of formal causes [or essences] is similar. For in the case of the intermediates, which have a posterior and a prior term, the prior must be of that which comes after it. For if we had to say which of the three is the cause, we should say the first; surely not the last, for the final is the cause of nothing; nor even the intermediate, for it is the cause only of one thing. But of series that are infinite in this way and of the infinite in general, all the parts including that which is now present are like intermediates; so that if there is no first, there is no cause at all. [. . .] Further, the final cause is an end and that sort of end that is not for the sake of something else, but for whose sake everything else is; so that if there is to be a last term of this sort, the process will not be infinite; but if there is no such term, there will be no final cause. [. . .] At the same time it is impossible that the primary existent, being eternal, should be destroyed. Since the upper creation is not limited, it is necessary that, not being eternal itself, it must be generated from something non-destroyed and primary. And since it is a final cause, it is the sort of thing that is not *for* other things; rather, other things are for *it*. Such a final cause there is, and no regress. Those who posit the infinite will, without realising this, have removed the nature of good.[9]

This Aristotelian proof is based on the following principles:[10]

1. The entities that be generated by the same origin possess a "foremost" which has an independent essence and is pre-eternal, and is the most complete and perfect form of the origin. Hence, motion

must be caused by an origin that is an Unmoved Mover; actuality, likewise, must return to a level of "actuality" that is pre-eternal, sheer actuality.
2. The chain of causes cannot infinitely regress:[11] since causality is a phenomenon that does take place in the world, its infinite regress is impossible.[12] Hence, there must be a First Cause.
3. Another issue of particular concern in this section is that the ultimate end does exist, and is one that all the ends are inclined to comprehend. That prime cause, the cause of all the other causes, the ultimate end, the mover who is not in motion, and sheer actuality, are different dimensions of the same entity, whom we know as God[13].

The Fourth Proof: The Principle of the Possibility of the Nobler

This principle explains the intelligible truth that whenever a less noble contingent entity exists, a nobler contingent entity must have preceded it in existence. In other words, the existence of a less noble contingent entity reveals the precedence of a nobler contingent entity. Therefore, the existence of a less noble contingent entity in the world of matter points to an ascending order that ends with the existence of God, who is Sheer Actuality and Absolute Being. This principle is found in an introductory format within the texts of Aristotle's works.

This entails a hierarchy of value and of truth. Contingent truths are predicated upon necessary truths. Investigating the causes of things is an inquiry into their truth. Thus the cause of causes is identified with the ultimate, necessary truth.

In the *Metaphysics*, Aristotle says:

"We do not know the truth without the cause. This is all the more true in each case in which synonymy arises, so that it is truer in each case that the earlier thing is the cause. And so it is necessary that the principles of the eternally existing things are most true so that, as each thing is related to being, so it is to truth. [. . .] A thing that imparts a certain characteristic to other things must itself enjoy a greater degree of the characteristic. Similarly, the cause of the truth of other things must be most true".[14]

Being, truth and causation are ontological scales within reality. In the above quote from Aristotle, we see that all limited perfection ultimately springs from the Absolute Perfect Being, the First Cause and the Ultimate End.

At least, this is how the text was interpreted in the late Antique intellectual traditions that came to influence Islam. The Neoplatonic account of Aristotle identified scales of perfection and reality; however, these concepts are not explicitly addressed in the Aristotelian corpus.[15]

The Fifth Proof: Knowledge and Thought

Because knowledge exists, and because its reality does not depend on an infinite series of entities, knowledge and thought necessarily possess a beginning and an end: that which is not infinite must of necessity be of a limited duration. Hence, the chain of existents, the weakest of which begins in matter, must end in sheer perfection, in the cause of all causes.

In his *Metaphysics*, Aristotle says:

However, neither can essence refer to another definition that is fuller in expression. For the original definition is always truer than the later one. And among the series of definitions, if the first definition lacks the intended characteristic, the next will do so likewise. This theory destroys knowledge. For it is impossible to have knowledge until one has reached the simple terms [that is, one has reached terms that cannot themselves be broken down into smaller or more simple parts]. And thus knowledge becomes impossible; for how is it possible to have cognition of infinite things? [. . .] But if the kinds of causes were infinite in number, knowledge would still be impossible. This is because we think that we have attained knowledge of something only when we have cognition of its causes; that which is infinite by addition cannot be gone through in a finite time.[16]

Therefore this chain of causes must have an end, since "knowledge" does exist.

The Sixth Proof: The Active Intellect

In contrast with Plato, Aristotle does not believe in the actual existence of intelligibles. Rather, he comprehends them as entities to be considered as the product of *sensibilia* and *imaginalia*; they are separable. The intellect itself becomes active while creating actual intelligibles. Hence, here too, in the actualization of the creation of the concepts, according to Aristotle's world of universal fundamental concepts, we must believe that the totality of potentiality comes from actuality, or matter from form, or the efficient cause from the influenced cause. In other words, we must believe in either two distinct intellects or two distinct dimensions of the intellect, one of which has been called, by commentators on Aristotelian philosophy, "the possible intellect" (*'aql mumkin*), "the influenced intellect" (*'aql munfa'il*), or "the active intellect" (*'aql fa'al*).[17]

Due to certain obscurities in the works of Aristotle, commentators have long disagreed in their interpretations of his views. Commentators can be divided into three different groups: the first and second groups consist of those who believe the active intellect to be separate and extrinsic to the human soul. These commentators are further sub-divided into two groups; first, those who, like Alexander of Aphrodisias, believe the active intellect to be the One God. Second, there are those who believe the active intellect to be caused by the metaphysical entities; it is outside the human soul, but not God.[18] This group, which includes al-Farabi (d. 950) and Avicenna (d. 1037), was known in the scholastic West as the Adherents of Averroes' (d. 1192). The third group, which believed in the unity of the intellect and its residence in the human being, are known as Thomists, after Thomas Aquinas (d. 1274), an early proponent of this view.

The discussion of the active intellect in the *De Anima* does not exceed sixteen lines[19] and Aristotle, in book Lambda of the *Metaphysics*, also mentions some of the characteristics of the active intellect.[20] In any case, if one holds, like Alexander of Aphrodisias, that the active intellect is the One God Himself, we have attained our objective. Nevertheless, even if we were to agree with the opinions of Averroes and Aquinas, we can demonstrate, through other proofs already mentioned (such as the principle of the possibility of the nobler, the impossibility of the chain of infinite causes, and by means of the existence of the active intellect), the necessity of the existence of God.

The Attributes of the Aristotelian Deity

1. The Prime Mover, who is not in motion, is Eternal and One.

Aristotle says in his *Physics*:

"Since motion is eternal, then the first mover, if there is but one, will be eternal also ... We do not need to assume that there are more than one".[21]

He then proves that motion is an eternal phenomenon, that it depends on a mover, and that the chain of movers must end at a mover which itself is unmoved, for infinite regress is impossible. Thus such an unmoved mover, which is the agent of eternal movement, must itself be eternal, for cause precedes the effect.[22]

In his *Metaphysics*, he says:

> "Since there were three kinds of substance, two of which are physical, and the third unmoved, regarding the latter we should say that there must be a kind of eternal unmoved substance. For substances are prior among existing entities, and if they are all destructible, all things are destructible. However, it is not possible that motion and time should either have come into being or cease to be, for these must always have existed".[23]

2. God is sheer actuality.

Aristotle, in the *Metaphysics*, says:

> "But suppose that there is something which is capable of moving things or acting on them, but is not actually doing so; there will not necessarily be movement, for that which has a potentiality need not exercise it. There is no advantage at all in the admission of eternal substances, as in the theory of Forms, unless there is among them a principle capable of moving something else. Not even this would be sufficient, and nor would another substance besides the Forms be sufficient; for, if it were not active, there could be no movement. Further, even if a Form could carry out an action, this would not be enough if its essence were potentiality. For there would not be eternal movement, since a potentially existing entity can also not exist. Thus, there must exist a principle the very essence of which is actuality".[24]

In book Zeta of the Metaphysics he says:

"[T]here is something which moves other entities without being moved, being eternal, substance and actuality"[25]

Further on he says:

"Substance is simple and exists actually"[26]

3. The Life of God

Having established that God is sheer actuality, Aristotle next must prove the life of God, for that which resides in the foremost station of actuality necessarily possesses the most intense degree of life and lives eternally.

"God also has life, since the actuality of thought is life, and He is that actuality. God's essential actuality is supreme, eternal life. We say, therefore, that God is a supreme and eternal living being, so that to God belongs life and continuous and eternal duration".[27]

4. God Has Knowledge of Himself Only

For Aristotle, the knowledge that God possesses cannot be knowledge that necessitates change or sensation; nor can it be noetic. Therefore, God, in the course of an eternal act, apprehends His own self-consciousness and comprehension. This is how Aristotle introduces God as the "Thinking of the Thought." God is that self-independent thought that contemplates eternally. Furthermore, God cannot have any object of thought beyond Himself, for that would mean that he has an end beyond Himself. Therefore, God only knows Himself.[28]

Concerning this, Aristotle says in the *Metaphysics*, book Lambda:

"The intrinsic object of thought is what is intrinsically best, and the intrinsic object of absolute thought is the absolutely best [i.e. God]".[29]).

5. God is Not the Creator, but the Ultimate Cause of the Universe

Greek thought did not posit creation. The world was considered to be pre-eternal; neither created in pre-eternity, nor dependent upon a creator. God is the first mover of the universe, and the source of eternal movement. He bestows upon the world a form, and, being the ultimate cause, invites the universe toward Himself—an act that is the source of motion in the universe. If God, as the efficient cause, had been the cause of motion, and controlled the universe, He would necessarily have had to undergo change. Thus, He is an agent, a final cause.[30]

6. God is Not Worshipped; Neither Does He Understand the Whisperings of His Servants

According to Aristotle, the Prime Mover is not the object of worship. He does not understand the worship and whisperings of His servants, since He has no knowledge of the deeds of His servants. In his *Magna Moralia*, Aristotle states:

"Those who think that God is someone who can be loved are mistaken, since God cannot attend to our love, and in no state can we say that we love God".[31]

Therefore, neither is God in communication with His servants, nor can man establish (any) communication with Him, through which He might behold the presence of humanity. The reason, according to Aristotle, is that this would result in a flaw in the sheer actuality of the ultimate cause that beholds no other than itself.

7. How Can the Multiplicity of Unmoved Movers Be Reconciled with Divine Unity?

In some of his works, Aristotle enumerates the number of unmoved movers to be 55 or so. On the other hand, he considers the unmoved mover to be God.[32] How can these two views concur—and how can they be reconciled with Divine unity?

In his *Metaphysics* Aristotle says:

"Although there are numerous unmoved movers, God is one, and one of these movers is the first".[33]

All Muslim philosophers and Christian scholastic philosophers believe that, according to Aristotle, God is one. They have propounded this view in numerous interpretations. Nonetheless, what is certain is that Aristotle does not explain how the numerous unmoved movers are linked to the first unmoved mover; this question remains ambiguous.

God in the Transcendent Philosophy of Mulla Sadra

Muhammad bin Ibrahim al-Qawami al-Shirazi (d. 1641), popularly known as Mulla Sadra, the founder of the school of thought known as Transcendent

Philosophy *(al-hikma al-muta'aliya)*, is well-known for having presented innovative philosophical principles.[34] Among these is his method for proving the existence of the Necessary Being, which is well-known as the "proof of the highly veracious" *(burhan al-siddiqin)*. He himself introduces it as the most apposite and sacred proof for the existence of God. Mulla Sadra, after briefly explaining that there exist different methods for proving the Necessary Being, introduces the method that he devised as the best, from which various other principles can also be drawn.

Transcendent Philosophy is the most important and exalted philosophical system, and it dominates Muslim philosophical circles, especially in Iran. After this school of thought was established in the 17th century, other notable philosophies (including the Peripatetic philosophy of Avicenna, the Illuminationist philosophy of Suhrawardi (d. 1191), the gnosis of Ibn 'Arabi, and scholastic theology) slowly came to be eclipsed by Mulla Sadra's system. His philosophy synthesized the significant points made by the four other philosophies listed above. Mulla Sadra's philosophy also provided profound new insights that were disseminated in those religious and intellectual circles open to philosophy and speculative theology; in such circles, his philosophy still prevails.

1. On Proving the Existence of a Necessary Being Through the "Proof of the Highly Veracious *(burhan al-siddiqin)*

Mulla Sadra, in his *Asfar*,[35] says:

> "Know that the paths that lead to Allah are numerous, because He possesses numerous virtues and dimensions. However, some of these are more firm, sacred and radiant than others. And the most apposite and sacred of proofs for His existence is that whose middle term, in reality, is none other than Himself. Hence, the path toward the objective is here the objective itself. And this is the path of the highly veracious *(siddiqin)*, who proves the existence of Allah through His exalted Self, and then proves His Attributes through His Essence, and His Acts through His Attributes, one after another. And others (such as the scholastic theologians [*mutakallimin*] and the materialists) seek knowledge of God and His Attributes through taking into consideration that which is other than Him [such as the contingency of essence *(mahiyyah)*, the createdness of creation, the motion of the material body, and other such matters]. These too are proofs of His Essence and

evidence of His Attributes; however, the former method is more firm and sacred.[36]

There are many ways of proving the existence of God, since God possesses ample virtues and numerous dimensions. However, some of these ways are more firm (*ahkam*), sacred (*ashraf*) and radiant (*anwar*) than others. The firmest and best proof of God's existence is a proof whose middle term (*hadd al-wasat*) is no other than the Necessary Being. This means that it is in contemplating the (nature of the) Divine Essence that we come to know of the existence of a Necessary Being, rather than by contemplating entities other than Him. Therefore, the path towards proving the existence of the Necessary Being is the Necessary being Himself. We reach our objective through our objective.

This is the method of the highly veracious (*siddiqun*), who, by contemplating the reality of existence, finds God, and, having proven the Divine Essence, proves His Attributes through His Essence, and His Acts through His Attributes, one after another. Those other than the *Siddiqin*, such as the scholastic theologians, materialists, and others, prove the Necessary Being by means of that which is other than God, such as the contingency of essence, the incipience (*huduth*) of the creation, the motion of the material body, and other such matters. These proofs of the existence of the Necessary Being also describe His Attributes. However, the method of the highly veracious is more firm and sacred.

A Brief Elucidation of the Proof of the Highly Veracious

> "The sages of the realm of Lordship (*al-rabbaniyyin*) behold existence and affirm its reality, and comprehend that it is fundamental in everything. Then, after [accurately] searching for the reality of existence, they realize that it is *necessarily* existent. As for contingency (*imkan*), need, effects (*ma'luliyyah*), and so on, they are attributed to it, not due to the nature of its reality, but because of the deficiencies and nonentities beyond the essence of its reality. Then, after contemplating that which necessitates essentiality (*wujub*) and contingency (*imkan*), they understand the unity of His Essence and Attributes, and likewise comprehend His Acts from His Attributes. And this is the method of the Prophets".[37]

The *rabbaniyyin* and divine scholars look at existence, study it, and come to understand that existence is the very nature of every entity. When they painstakingly search for the reality of existence, they find that that the reality of existence is necessary in its essence; sheer existence is the Necessary Being. The reality of existence in itself is free from imperfection and is not exposed to contingency, need or effects. However, in case of its imperfection, it is dependent.

A lower degree of existence, however, is contingent; otherwise, existence itself is neither dependent nor contingent. Then, taking into consideration the necessary consequence of *necessity* and *contingency*, and understanding that completeness is inherent in *necessity*, and that the Necessary Being possesses no imperfection, they conclude that the Necessary Being possesses no partner in His Essence and Attributes. This is the method of the Prophets.

Having briefly expounded the "proof of the highly veracious," Mulla Sadra presents the same in a logical format, based on the following four premises:[38]

1. The fundamentality of existence (*asalat al-wujud*)
2. The unity (*wahid*) and not the heterogeneity (*mutabayin*) of existence
3. The graduation (*tashkik*) of existence
4. The simplicity (*bisata*) of existence

A Logical Exposition of the Proof of the Highly Veracious

> Indeed [concrete] existence, as explained earlier, is a single (*wahidah*) and simple (*basitah*) tangible reality, whose extensions (*afrad*) have no difference, save in perfection and imperfection, strength and weakness, or in additional matters (*umur za'idah*), as is the case with the extensions of a generic essence (*mahiyyah naw'iyyah*). The ultimate perfection of existence is that which cannot be surpassed in completeness, and that which does not depend on others. And what surpasses it in completeness cannot be comprehended, for every imperfect entity depends on other than itself, and is in need of completeness; and, as was made clear earlier, completeness precedes incompleteness, actuality precedes potentiality, and existence precedes non-existence. It is likewise clear that the completeness of a thing is the thing itself, and what is in addition to itself. Hence, existence is either independent of other than itself, or it is essentially dependent on other than itself. The former among these two is the Necessary Being and Sheer Existence, whom nothing can surpasses in completeness. Nor does any kind of nullity and imperfection stain Him; and the latter are all

existents other than Him, such as His Acts and Effects, and there is no support for anything other than Him, save what is in Him.[39]

Here is a summary of the above-mentioned proof of the highly veracious:

According to the fundamentality of existence,

Premise 1: Because concrete existence is fundamental and real,
Premise 2: and because it is one (*wahid*), and not heterogeneous (*mutabayin*),
Premise 3: and because it has a gradated unity (*wahdah tashkikiyya*) and not an individual [hypostatic] unity (*wahdah shakhsiyya*),
Premise 4: and because of its simplicity (*bisata*), and the fact that its plurality reverts to its unity, meaning that all its pluralities and distinctions revert to existence (this exposition in reality portrays the very spirit of the gradation of existence, even though it is discussed in a different context from that of gradation),

Conclusion: therefore, we say that every entity is either Necessary or reliant upon a Necessary Being. If it were Sheer existence and possessed the highest degree (of existence, and no imperfection could be comprehended in it (meaning that it did not depend on other than itself), it would then be Necessary; however, if it was not Sheer Existence, but imperfect, it would essentially depend on Sheer Existence.

Mulla Sadra then provides a short reminder that the essence of the proof of the highly veracious states that the reality of existence is the very Necessary Being; this establishes a basis for proving the Oneness of God and other Attributes of His Essence and Beautiful Names. By means of the proof of the highly veracious, not only can the Necessary Being itself be proved, but His Unity and other Attributes can likewise be established.

In this short reminder in the *Asfar*, Mulla Sadra says:

The light of truth has dawned on the horizon of this exposition [the proof of the highly veracious] which has pricked up your ears . . . That is, Sheer Existence is not attributed to deficiency and inability due to its simplicity (for, save existence, there is nothing to add to existence to necessitate its composition), and neither does it depend on an existential support, nor possess an essential definition (*muhaddad mahuwi*). Hence, that reality is the very Necessary Being that possesses the highest degree of perfection, the intensity of which is without end. [. . .] Every degree [of existence] other than the highest degree is not Sheer Existence, but a nonentity; and existence in its sheer-ness has no shortcoming or deficiency; rather, whenever it is an effect (*ma'lul*) and "unknown" (*majhul*), it is imperfect and inadequate. Imperfection and inadequacy are the essence of the secondary stages of existence, and not the essence of existence [in the absolute sense.[40]

This is where the logical exposition of the proof of the highly veracious, which establishes the existence of the Necessary Being, ends.

2. God's Oneness is Not Numerical

> Imperfection and inadequacy are the essential [properties] of the secondary stages of existence, and not essential to existence itself. "Secondary stages" does not mean the existents that reside in the second stage of existence. Rather, "secondary" here refers to "that which is not the first," even though it may be in the third or fourth stage of existence. The Almighty Necessary Being Who is the First Absolutely Absolute is Sheer Existence, and free from imperfection, and does not possess any essential definition. He is not made, nor created, and nothing more complete than Him can be imagined. An imperfect and poor entity is the result of effusion (*ifjxah*) and concoction (*ja'l*).[41]

The important point made in the above quotation is that the word "first," when applied to the Necessary Being, does not mean that He possesses a "second," for He is that first whose second is the very first. Hence, a series of numbers such as "first" and "second" does not apply to Him. The concept of numbers is a distinction that belongs to the world of contingency, and is found in the lower stage of effusion (*fayd*).

3. **Proving the Oneness of the Necessary Being**

> Indeed, the existence of a Necessary Being has been proven by this demonstration, and by it, His Unity is also established, since existence is one reality, which, due to its nature and essence, cannot be susceptible to imperfection—and no multiplicity can be conceived in his Infinity.[42]

In reality, Mulla Sadra derives the Oneness of the Necessary Being from the essence of the "proof of the highly veracious," since it has been established that the Exalted Necessary Being is Sheer Existence and Utter Reality, and not an existence admixed with imperfection and need; and also because of the fact that "a thing in itself cannot be replicated."

Since the Necessary Being is Infinite, and since thus it is impossible for any alterity to stand beside it, there is no reason to assume its multiplicity. A pure and infinite entity is sheer infinity. That is, not only does it not possess a partner, but there exists no alterity beyond Himself, since He is Infinite and there is no other space that could be occupied by another entity. If another being could be imagined, both beings would be limited, and thus neither could be necessary.

Obviously, the emanations (*fuyudat*) that exist in the universe cannot be other than God; rather, they are His manifestations and signs; they are facets and degrees of that Sacred Entity.

Divine Attributes in Transcendent Philosophy

1. Universal Discussions Pertaining to Divine Attributes

The discussion of Divine Attributes in Sadraian philosophy is of two kinds: (1) a discussion of universals (*kulliyyat*), and (2) a discussion of particulars (*juz'iyyat*).[46]

As is the case with general metaphysics, where a series of complete and all-inclusive discussions forming the primary issues are propounded at the outset, the discussion of the attributes of the Necessary being is likewise preceded by similar discussions. That is, the first to be discussed are universal issues relating to the subject. This includes the attribute (*sifah*) and its difference from the name (*ism*), the distinction of each from the Essence, the division of attributes into positive (*thubuti*), negative (*salbi*), essential (*dhati*), active (*fi'li*), intellectual (*'aqli*) and sensory (*hissi*), the relation of the attribute and the Essence, the correlation of the attributes with one another, their reversion to a single attribute and vice versa, and the judgment of the reversion. Then, specific Divine attributes are discussed.

2. Classifications of the Attributes

Mulla Sadra says in the *Asfar*:

> An attribute is either positive (*ijbiyyah*) or negative (*salbiyyah*) and sacred (*taqdisiyyah*) . . . God in the Holy Qur'an is qualified as

"the Possessor of Majesty and Splendor,"[47] (*dhi l-jalal wa l-ikram*), meaning that the most sacred Divine Essence is more exalted than others, and, in having the attributes of Beauty and Perfection, possesses Splendor (*karama*).[43]

The verse "None is as His Likeness" (Qur'an, al-Shura [42], v. 11) includes all of the negative and majestic attributes of Almighty God, and [also] embraces all of the positive and beautiful attributes of Almighty God . . . "And Allah's are the most beautiful Names" (Qur'an, al-A'raf, v. 180).

3. The Negative Attributes

Mulla Sadra says in the *Asfar*:

> "The first group (of Attributes) are negative and majestic, which negate deficiency and nihility, and all of the negative attributes return to one negation; and that is the negation of contingency [from His Exalted Essence]".[44]

This is because all deficiencies and nonentities revert to contingency. This statement of Mulla Sadra's clarifies three things:

1. That which is negated (*maslub*) by negative attributes is the non-existence or deficiency of the Divine Essence.
2. All negations revert to one negation.
3. That negation is the negation of contingency.

What is meant by contingency, according to the rest of the philosophers, is the contingency of essence (*imkan mahuwi*), while Mulla Sadra believes it to be "the contingency of deficiency" (*imkan faqri*).

The Real (*haqiqi*) and Relational (*idafi*) Attributes, Positive (*thubuti*) or Actual (*fi'li*)

The second group (of attributes) are the positive attributes, and the attributes of beauty, which are subdivided into "real" and "relational." The real attributes are those in which "a relation with other than His Essence" is not taken into consideration, such as life and the knowledge the Essence has about Himself; whereas a relational (or actual) attribute is that in which a connection with "other than the Divine Essence" is taken into consideration, such as creation (*khaliqiyyah*), sustenance (*raziqiyyah*), and so on. Each of these cannot be deduced from the Essence alone; rather, in deducing them, another entity, together with the Essence, must be considered.

Mulla Sadra in his *Asfar* says:

The second group is classified into "real attributes" such as knowledge and life, and "relational attributes" such as creation, sustenance, precedence, and causality (*'illiyyah*). And the source of all the real (or positive) attributes is the necessity of existence—i.e., the emphasized existence (*wujud mu'akkad*)—whereas the source of all the relational attributes is a relational attribute which is itself the relational attribute of (existential) preponderance (*qayyumiyyah*).[45]

4. Returning the Multiplicity of the Attributes to the Oneness of the Essence

Mulla Sadra says in the *Asfar*:

> "Verify it here in this way, so that by bringing back all the multiplicities to One, the One reality of the Necessary being would not break up; for God is loftier than that the sanctuary of His simplicity, and Sheer-ness is destroyed by the entry of multiplicity".[46]

5. The Difference Between Attributes of the Essence and Attributes of Act

Mulla Sadra in his *Asfar* says:

In the same way as all the real attributes of the Necessary Being are a single reality, and not additional to His Essence (although the concepts [*mafhumat*] of the attributes are distinct, otherwise these terms would be synonymous), all the relational attributes of the Necessary being are likewise one relation, posterior to the Essence and additional to it, even through they conceptually differ from one another.[47]

What Mulla Sadra means by this is that the distinction between the attributes of the Essence and the attributes of act is not that of unity and multiplicity, since both the source of the attributes of the Essence and the attributes of act themselves refer to a singular reality. The only distinction between them is whether they possess unity or are an addition to the Essence.

6. God's Attributes are His Very Essence

Mulla Sadra, in the first section (al-*mashhad al-awwal*) and the third emanation (*ishraq*) of al-*Shawahid al-Rububiyyah*, says the following on this issue:

> The attributes of the Necessary Being are not additional to His Essence, but rather the existence of the Necessary Being is this very Essence; it is, in its reality, a manifestation of all the attributes of perfection, without necessitating multiplicity (*kathra*), passivity (*infi'al*), acceptance (*qabul*) and activity (*fi'l*) in His Essence. And the difference between His Essence and His Attributes is like the difference between existence and the essence of the entities that possess essence (meaning that the attributes are the detailed level of the Essence, in the manner that essence in contingent entities is the specification and definition of the degree of essence of the entity), except for the fact that the Necessary Being has no quiddity, for He is sheer I-ness
> (*inniyyah*), from whose beginning-less source have sprung the rest of the I-nesses (*inniyyat*) and existents. Thus, in the manner that existence in its essence and in its reality is existent, and essence in itself and its essence is non-existent, but rather gains existence by means of existence, likewise the Divine attributes and names are, in themselves and in their essential meanings, non-existent; rather, they exist in the sense of the reality of simplicity (*haqiqat al-ahadiyya*) (which means the absorption of the names and attributes in the (exalted) state of the Essence.[48]

The Seven Essential Attributes: "The Seven Leaders"

The principal attributes of God—Life, Knowledge, Power, Will, Hearing, Seeing and speech—are called "the seven leaders." Of these some call life, knowledge, and power, the positive attributes of the Essence, and hearing, sight, and speech, the attributes of act. Our philosopher has propounded the attribute of God's love for his creation too, both in the *Asfar* and the *Shawahid*.

7. The Power and Knowledge of the Necessary Being: His Essence

Mulla Sadra, in his *Shawahid*, says:

> "The power of the Necessary Being is the emanation of entities from His Essence, by sheer will, the will that is the very Essence, and not an addition to the Essence. And the knowledge the Necessary Being has of His own Essence, which is this very pre-eternal consideration, is the revelation of His Essence for the Essence, in a manner in which all the good and virtues emanate from His Essence for His Essence [meaning that His Essence is the beginning and real source of all virtues, perfections, and excellences of existence]".[49]

The point that must be noted concerning Divine power is that it is infinite, and embraces every contingent entity. However, the potentiality of an entity does not necessitate its existence, and only those things come into being that God intends. In other words, being powerful does not mean that one can do anything. Rather, it means that one can do whatever He intends. Hence, essential impossibilities (*muhalat-i dhati*) are outside the sphere of things that His power can bring about, and the question of whether they can be created by God's power is absurd. On the other hand, not all contingent entities are intended by God; not all of these come into existence. Thus, the scope of the existents and entities intended by God is narrower than that of the entities that can be created by Him.[50]

8. The Knowledge the Necessary Being Has About That Which Other Than Himself

Mulla Sadra, in al-*Mabda' wa al-Ma'ad*, classifies those who believe that the Necessary has knowledge about other than Himself into eight groups.[51] Among these are the Mu'tazila, a group of Sufi masters who adhere to the teachings of Plato, Shaykh al-Ishraq [Suhrawardi], a group of Peripatetic philosophers such as al-Farabi, Avicenna, Porphyry, and others. Mulla Sadra investigates their views, which he critiques as incomplete. Thereafter he expounds his own opinion, and says:

> "The evidence that the Almighty Necessary Being has knowledge of His Essence, necessitates that He also has knowledge of all the existents of the Universe, for His Essence is the necessitating cause (*'illah mujibah*) of every thing, and the origin of every comprehension, be it intellectual or sensory. Likewise [it] is [also] the source of the manifestation of every entity, be it mental or external. And all of these entities, directly or through mediation, emanate from Him. Complete knowledge of the necessitating

cause necessitates complete knowledge of the effect of the said cause, and this necessitates that the Almighty Necessary Being knows all the existents, and the Holy Qur'an says: "Doesn't that Who created Know, while He is the All-Subtle and All-Aware" [(Qur'an, al-Mulk [67], v.14.)] It says, does not the Creator have knowledge? This means that He is the cause of the effects and at the same time a being who is All-Subtle, i.e., non-corporeal (*mujarrad*), and All-Aware, i.e., "He has knowledge of His Essenc."[52]

He continues by saying:

> Know that as His perfection in causing things is due to the completeness of His existence, and His intensity of possession is to the extent that all existents and good emanate from him, and not only that all entities are attributed to Him and are related to Him; that is, this relative meaning is not meant, for this understates the degree of His existence, magnificence, and sublimity; rather, the ultimate end behind the bestowal of grace and causation is His very Sacred Essence; and He is Needless of other than Himself; likewise, His perfection in His knowledge is not merely that the essences of things or their forms are in His presence, which would mean that their essences and intellectual forms were not of the same degree as His Essence but rather, inferior to His Essence, which is the case in reality. This would necessitate His lack of perfection to a degree inferior to His Essence, which would in turn necessitate that He could only gain perfection by means of other than Himself, after being imperfect in His Essence—but Allah is far exalted from such a condition.[53]

9. The Life of the Necessary Being

Having proven the knowledge and power of God, the concomitant of the two, which is life, is also established. Furthermore, it is impossible for a cause that bestows existence to lack the perfection that it bestows upon its creation.

Mulla Sadra, in his *Asfar*, says the following concerning the life of the Almighty Necessary Being:

> "The life that we possess in this world is actualized through comprehension and action. And comprehension with relation to

most animals is none other than sensation. And such is also the case with action, which is none other than spatial movement (*al-tahrik al-makani*), which originates with an urge. These two effects spring from two different faculties: one of these is the faculty of comprehension (*mudrikah*), and the other is the faculty of execution (*muharrikah*). Therefore, if one should possess a faculty of comprehension more sacred than sensation, such as intellection (*ta'aqqul*) and the like, and if it should produce action beyond spatial movement, such as creation and the like, this should be referred to as "life." Furthermore, if the very origin of comprehension were also the origin of action, without [there being] any difference [between the two], so that its very comprehension would likewise be its action and creation, this should also be referred to with this name, due to its purity. That is, it has not been composed in the usual sense, for composition necessitates contingency and fallibility, due to the dependence of the composite entity on a substance other than itself. Contingency is a form of nihility (*'adam*), which is the opposite of existence, and death is the opposite of life, and extinction is the opposite of subsistence. Thus, the truly living entity is that which has not been composed; and it has been verified that the Necessary Being is a Simple reality, single in Essence and Attribute, the sole possessor of power and strength, and that His very comprehension of entities is their emanation from Him. He is Singular and Simple in that he is the universal intellect and the origin of every entity. Hence it is he who possesses the true essence of life rather than any living entity. Why not, since He is the Giver of life, the Bestower of Existence, and the perfection of existence, knowledge and power, compared to any mere possessor of existence, knowledge and power?"[54]

10. The Will of the Almighty Necessary Being

"Will" is used in two senses: one is to love, and the other is to decide. To love and decide to carry out one's own voluntary action is called the generative will (*irada-yi takwini*), and to love and decide that another agent should performs a voluntary act is known as the legislative will (*irada-yi tashri'i*). However, the will to issue a command and establish law is the will to legislate (*irada-yi tashri'*), and not the legislative will (*irada-yi tashri'i*); legislation itself is a generative (*takwini*) act.

For this reason, the divine generative will can be understood in two senses: one is the sense of love toward his own voluntary acts, which is a simple, pre-eternal, essential attribute, and is identical to the essence Whose relation to actions and objective entities is like essential knowledge: it is of the sacred divine essence, and subordinately, of His effects. Likewise, divine love is basically directed toward His own sacred essence and, subordinately, toward the effects of His existence that overflow from the Divine goodness and perfection; and this is why it is known as will.[55] Mulla Sadra, in section six of his *al-Mabda' wa l-Ma'ad*, elucidates the above summary.

11. The Hearing and Vision of the Almighty Necessary Being

God is the All-Hearing, meaning that he has unmediated and direct knowledge *('ilm huduri)* of auditories and He is (also) All-Seeing; that is, He has unmediated and direct knowledge of visibilities. And this is what "*huwa al-sami'al basir*" (He is the All-Hearing and the All-Seeing) actually means.

After analyzing and critiquing the views of Shaykh Abu l-hasan al-Ash'ari (d. 935) and Nasir al-Din Tusi (d. 1274) in his *Asfar* and al-*Mabda' wa l-Ma'ad*, Mulla Sadra establishes his own view in the following manner:

The concepts of audition and vision are other than the concept of knowledge; and these two are a particular kind of knowledge additional to knowledge in the absolute sense.[56]

He establishes that the condition of inclusion (*manat al-juzi'yyat*) is either sensation (which is impossible without a medium), or illuminative intuition (*mashhud ishraqi*), which is not incongruous with immateriality from body and purity from matter. And he also establishes that God knows all the particular entities in their particular and material characteristics, out of which there are auditories such as the letters and sounds, and visibilities such as the radiant and colourful bodies. Hence God's knowledge about all of these entities is illuminative (*ishraqi*) and presential *(hudhuri)*; and it is an intuitive and radiant disclosure that is grasped by itself. Hence His Essence is audition and vision in this respect without any interpretation (*ta'wil*).

Hence, if it is said that the knowledge of the Almighty Necessary Being returns to His Sight, and not that His Sight returns to His Absolute Knowledge, this is better and nearer to the truth, as has been said by sahib al-ishraq [Suhrawardi].[57]

A Critical Comparison Between the Views of Aristotle and Mulla Sadra

1. Proof for the Existence of God

The most important and well-known proof Aristotle provides for the existence of One God (the very "oneness" of which is obscure as we have said), is the proof of motion (*burhan al-haraka*), from which we come to know of a prime unmoved mover. This proof possesses characteristics that we discuss here.

Firstly, in itself, it is not a proof of the existence of God, but rather, a proof of the existence of a metaphysical realm.
Secondly, it depends on the impossibility of infinite regress.
Thirdly, one can perceive shortcomings in some its premises, especially taking into consideration the view propounded by Modern Physics on the law of gravity in movement.
Fourthly, the Cause is understood by means of effect and other entities.
Fifthly, it rests on several premises.

By sharp contrast, the path traversed by Mulla Sadra in proving the Necessary Being, known as the Proof of the Highly Veracious surpasses the proof of motion in various ways:

Firstly, we come to know that the exalted Creator is a Necessary Existent Being in the reality of existence.
Secondly, by contemplating existence we find that God is peerless, and leaves no room for other than Himself, so that no peer may be presumed for Him.
Thirdly, the rest of the attributes of God are established from the centre of this very path.
Fourthly, it does not depend on the impossibility of infinite regress or a vicious circle.
Fifthly, there is no need to consider the middle term to be other than Almighty God to prove the existence of Almighty God.

Mulla Sadra, in his *Asfar* and *Shawahid*, explains the reasons for the superiority of the Proof of the Highly Veracious over the other proofs for the existence of the Almighty Necessary Being, as follows:

> This path that we have traversed is the firmest and most sacred of paths, for in order to know the Essence, Attributes, and Acts of the

Almighty Necessary Being, it is not necessary to place any other entity as the middle term (*hadd awsat*), nor need we depend on nullifying infinite regress or the vicious circle. Rather, we can know, from the reality of existence, the existence of the Necessary Being, which is (also) the reality of existence, and from, the Oneness of the Almighty Being. [. . .] From the core of this path, the signs and acts of God are also known. However, not everyone possesses a powerful aptitude to infer ample laws from the fundamental facet of unity. Hence, other ways must also be shown, although none of these paths, save this, allows the spiritual traveller (*salik*) reach the ultimate end.[58]

According to the late 'Allamah Tabataba'i in his gloss on the *Asfar* on this very discussion, all of the proofs for the existence of Almighty God have an exhortative (*tanbihi*) dimension, due to the fact that the existence of the Almighty God is a pre-eternal and essential issue, and means the existence of the reality, which is the border line between sophistry and philosophy.

2. The Aristotelian God is a Deistic God, and Mulla Sadra's God is a Theistic God

This is one of the most important differences between the God of Aristotle and the God of Mulla Sadra, for deism is belief in God without accepting a religion. This belief-system holds that divine attributes are quite separate from the divine essence that is the cause of the cosmos and the cosmos itself. However, a divine being does not have a direct effect on events, which, in fact, leaves no room for the existence of relations between man and God. On the other hand, theism stands for belief and acceptance of religion, which is a direct relationship between human entities and the world.

3. The Knowledge of the Necessary Being About Other Than Himself

Aristotle considers that this would entail imperfection and defect in the Divine Essence. In sharp contrast, Mulla Sadra holds the contrary, and presents those who believe that God's knowledge does not comprehend other than His Essence as ignorant.

Of course, this is a subtle and difficult issue of philosophical theology that Mulla Sadra, as mentioned above, proves by means of his unique method, a summary of which is as follows:

God's knowledge about His Essence is according to His Essence, and not something else. Hence, he would also have the same essential knowledge that is according to the Essence. Thus, because His Essence Itself is the origin of the knowledge of all the entities, and by Its disclosure to Itself, all the other entities with their essences are divulged to His Essence, even though, in consideration of the knowledge of the entities, they are in a degree posterior to the Knowledge of the Essence.[59]

4. Audition and vision

In Aristotelian philosophy, due to the reason that God has no knowledge of other than Himself, He is not All-Hearing or All-Seeing. However, in Transcendent Philosophy God does possess knowledge of other than His Essence. God is All-Hearing (*Sami'*), which means that he has presential knowledge about auditories (*masmu'at*), and is All-Seeing (*Basir*), meaning that he has presential knowledge about visibilities (*mubsirat*).

However, due to the fact that Mulla Sadra

1. does not consider God's Attention to that which is other than Himself to necessitate imperfection in His Essence,
2. comprehends all the existents to be attributed to God,
3. and holds that God ardently loves His Essence;
4. consequently, He also loves the effects that emanate from His Essence.
5. In fact, the love of God for His servants is based on at least four premises that have been established in Transcendental Philosophy, and Mulla Sadra, based on these pre-established premises, is strengthened in his view.

Mulla Sadra in his *Shawahid* starts his proof with the verse of the Holy Qur'an that says "He loves them, and they love Him" and says:

"The Sacred Essence of the Necessary Being is an Entity Whose happiness and delight for His own Essence is of the highest degree of intensity. This is because in the state of Self-comprehension, He is the greatest being who comprehends, in the highest degree of comprehension, Himself, and He is the most beautiful of all existents; and the knower (*'alim*), the known (*ma'lum*) and knowledge (*'ilm*), are the same as His Essence; also, all of the three are of the highest in their levels and degrees. In sensory beings, pleasure means the comprehension of a perfection that reaches the power of sensation;

no veil exists. However, that meaning of pleasure is apposite for the level of the Necessary Being, although pleasure in that sense is not (normally) referred to as pleasure, but rather as joy (*bahjah*) and sublimity ('*ala*'). Therefore, the Necessary Being is a superior and more exalted being who ardently loves His own essence as well as the entities other than His Essence. This love has no bounds in its intensity, for, one who is the ardent lover of another, is (also) an ardent lover of every thing related to himself, because of the (very) relation. Earlier in the discussion of existence it was proven to you and known that the self-existence (*wujud fi nafsih*) of every entity that emanates from the Necessary Being and is attributed to His Essence, is the very existence and emanation of the Necessary Being, without there being any difference between the two existents."[60]

The love of God's creatures for the Necessary Being is as follows: first, the Almighty Necessary Being placed ardent love in all the entities of the universe, including the human being. The most intense degree of this ardent love is in man.

Second, since God is All-Hearing and All-Seeing and possesses knowledge of other than Himself, He comprehends the love of His servants and receives the same.

Mulla Sadra in his *Shawahid* says:

No entity exists that does not possess a perfection that it seeks, or a volitional or a natural love peculiar to itself, or a voluntary or innate desire and impulse that leads it to attain perfection when it separates from the same; and this is his share of the sacred grace, which is a mercy on him from the Lord of pre-eternal providence.[61]

6. The God of Aristotle is not a Creator, Whereas Mulla Sadra's God is a Creator

Generally, in Greek thought, there is no discourse on creation; and Aristotle, too, from the very beginning considers the world to be pre-eternal. A theology of creation is very much a product of a monotheistic perspective. Nevertheless, in the Sadrian philosophy too, both God and the universe are pre-eternal. However, the universe is a creation of God, and dependent in its entirety upon a Being who is Independent.

7. The Attributes of Act

The God of Mulla Sadra has positive and actual attributes. However, the God of Aristotle has no such attributes (such as audition, vision, speech, creation, sustenance). The God of Aristotle has no knowledge of the present world, and he unfolds no divine design or providence. Hence, in short, the God of Aristotle compared to that of Mulla Sadra is very primitive, both in his God's existence and His attributes.

Conclusion

The God of Mulla Sadra, single, and cognizant only of His essence, is a sophisticated and rich concept. As the highest degree of existence, He is sheer existence, absolute perfection, the efficient, ultimate, and sufficient cause, the creator, God, and beloved of the inhabitants of the universe; and God's grace is pre-eternal and eternal. He is aware of all the apparent and hidden secrets of the world.

The God of Aristotle is the prime unmoved mover, the ultimate cause, sheer actuality, eternal, beautiful God of Mulla Sadra. He is the first existent, the complete entity—even more exalted than "completeness" and "perfection." He is a God who does not lack any perfection or attributes of perfection. He is an entity who is complete actuality, is prior to every other entity, is one and absolute, is simple from every dimension, is actuality from every side, and His essence possesses all the attributes of perfection.

Bibliography

Amuli, Javad. *Sharh-i Asfar-i Arba'a*. Tehran: Intisharat-i al-Zahra, 1996.
Aristotle, 1984. *The Complete Works*. Edited by J. Barnes. Princeton: Princeton University Press.
Aristotle. *Aristotelis Fragmenta Selecta*. Edited by W.D. Ross. Oxford: Clarendon Press, 1955
Aristotle. *Physics*. Translated by R. Waterfield. London: Penguin, 1996.
Aristotle. *The Metaphysics*. Translated by H. Tancred-Lawson. London: Penguin, 1998.
Aristotle. *On the Soul [De Anima]*. Translated by H. Tancred-Lawson. London: Penguin, 1999.
Armstrong, A.H. *An Introduction to Ancient Philosophy*. London: Methuen & Co, 1947.

Barnes, J. ed. *The Cambridge Companion to Aristotle*. Cambridge: Cambridge University Press, 1995.
Barnes, J. et al. eds., 1975-9. *Articles on Aristotle*. London: Duckworth.
Barnes, J. *Aristotle: A Very Short Introduction*. Oxford: Oxford University Press, 1999.
Blumenthal, H. "Neoplatonic Elements in the de Anima Commentaries." In: R. Sorabji, ed. *Aristotle transformed*. London: Duckworth, pp. 305-24, 1990.
Cooper, J."Mulla Sadra Shirazi." In: E. Craig, ed. *The Routledge Encyclopaedia of Philosophy*. London: Routledge, 1998, pp. 595-99.
Davoodi, 'Ali Murad. *'Aql dar hikmat-i mashsha'i*. Tehran: Intisharat-i Dehkhoda, 1349 sh.
Davidson, H.A. *Proofs for Eternity, Creation and the Existence of God in Medieval Islamic and Jewish Philosophy*. New York: Oxford University Press, 1987.
Fowden, G. *From Empire to Commonwealth: Consequences of Monotheism in Late Antiquity*. Princeton: Princeton University Press, 1993.
Gerson, L. *God and Greek Philosophy: Studies in the Early History of Natural Theology*. London: Routledge, 1991.
Leaman, O. *An Introduction to Medieval Islamic Philosophy*. Cambridge: Cambridge University Press,1985.
Lloyd, A.C. "The Principle that the Cause is Greater than the Effect." *Phronesis*, 21, 1976, pp. 146-56.
Misbah Yazdi, M.T. *Philosophical Instructions (Amuzesh-i falsafa)*. Translated by M. Legenhausen and A. Sarvdalir. Binghamton: SSIPS with Global Publications, Binghamton University, 1999.
Morris, J. *The Wisdom of the Throne*. Princeton: Princeton University Press, 1981.
Nasr, S.H. and O. Leaman eds. *History of Islamic Philosophy*. London: Routledge, 1996.
Netton, I. *Allah Transcendent*. Richmond: Curzon Press, 1994.
Rahman, F. *The Philosophy of Mulla Sadra*. Albany: State University of New York Press, 1975.
Shirazi, Mulla Sadra. *al-Hikma al-muta'aliya fi l-asfar al-'aqliyya al-arba'a*. 3rd ed. Beirut: Dar ihya' al-turath al-'arabi, vol 6, 1981.
Shirazi, Mulla Sadra. *al-Mabda' wa l-ma'ad*. ed. Ashtiyani, S.J. Tehran: Imperial Iranian Academy of Philosophy, 1976.
Shirazi, Mulla Sadra,. *al-Shawahid al-rububiyya*. ed. Ashtiyani, S.J. Mashhad: Mashhad University Press, 1967.
Shirazi, Mulla Sadra. *The Metaphysics of Mulla Sadra (al-Masha'ir)*. Translated by P. Morewedge. New York: SSIPS, 1992.

Owens, J. *The Doctrine of Being in the Aristotelian Metaphysics*. Toronto: Pontifical Institute of Mediaeval Studies, 1978.

Ziai, H. 'Mulla Sadra: His life and works', in Nasr and Leaman, ed, *History of Islamic Philosophy*, pp. 635-642. London: Routledge, 1996.

Endnotes:

1. There is an ongoing debate about whether there really is any theology in Aristotle: is he merely a secular thinker whose discourse of 'god' or 'gods' is a certain *façon de parler*, or is he serious proto-Thomist or Avicennan thinker who mediates on such matters? See Barnes, *Aristotle*, pp. 102-4; Owens, *The Doctrine of Being in the Aristotelian Metaphysics*, pp. 49-62.
2. Henotheism is the belief in a paramount and single, but not exclusive, god.
3. Fowden, *From Empire to Commonwealth: Consequences of Monotheism in Late Antiquity*, pp. 5-11.
4. See Aristotle, *The Metaphysics*, 1072a, pp. 21-26; Aristotle, Physics, 241b ff; Barnes, *The Cambridge Companion to Aristotle*, pp. 104-5. For some useful discussions on this topic, see Verbeke 1969, Easterling 1970, Lang 1978, Ackrill 1991, Davidson 1987, and Gerson 1991. This proof was articulated early on in Islamic philosophy by al-Kindi (d. after 866)—see al-Kindi [1998]. See also Netton, *Allah Transcendent*. For a discussion of proofs from motion in Islam, see Davidson, *Proofs for Eternity*.
5. See Aristotle, *The Metaphysics*, pp. 167-231, *Metaphysics* 1072a-1073a, pp. 373-75.
6. Cf. Gerson, *God and Greek Philosophy*, pp. 116-17 and Aristotle, *The Metaphysics*, 242a, pp. 49-57; 258b, pp. 10-12; 259a, pp. 6-12.
7. Aristotle, *The Metaphysics*, 1998, 1049b, 18-25; Barnes 1995, pp. 94-96.
8. Mulla Sadra, *al-Mabda' wa l-ma'ad*, p. 11.
9. Aristotle, *The Metaphysics* 1998, 994a-b, pp. 45-7.
10. For a discussion of this proof and its cognate proof in Islamic systematic theology (*kalam*), see Davidson, *Proofs for Eternity*, 1987, pp. 117-27, pp. 336ff, pp. 407-8.
11. This is an Aristotelian axiom—see Aristotle, *Posterior Analytics I.3*; see also Smith, "Logic," in *The Cambridge Companion to Aristotle*, p. 57.
12. Because infinites cannot exist in causal reality, but can only be mentally posited.
13. Aristotle, *The Metaphysics*, 1998, 1037a 6, p. 209; Owens 1978, p. 171.
14. Aristotle, *The Metaphysics*, 1998, 993b-994a, pp. 44-5.
15. There is, however, an Aristotelian fragment from his *On Philosophy*, reported by Simplicius, that argues from the imperfect to the perfect:
In general among things where there is a better, there is also a best. Since, then, among existing things one is better than another, there is also something that is best, which will be divine.

16. Aristotle, *The Metaphysics,* 1998, 994b, p. 47.
17. Davoodi, *'Aql dar hikmat-i mashsha'i,* 1349 sh., p. 80.
18. Blumenthal, "Neoplatonic Elements in the de Anima Commentaries." In: R. Sorabji, ed. *Aristotle transformed.* 1990, pp. 312-321.
19. Aristotle, *On the Soul,* 1999, pp. 204-5; Gerson, 1991, pp. 122-23.
20. Aristotle, *The Metaphysics,* 1998, 1074b-1075a, pp. 382-83.
21. Aristotle, *Physics,* 1996, 259a 6-12, p. 209.
22. Cf. Lloyd 1976, pp. 146-56.
23. Aristotle, *The Metaphysics,* 1998, 1071b, pp. 368-69; Cf. Gerson, *God and Greek Philosophy,* 1991, p. 121.
24. Aristotle, *The Metaphysics,* 1998, 1071b, p. 369; Cf. Gerson, *God and Greek Philosophy,* 1991, pp. 124-5.
25. Aristotle, *The Metaphysics,* 1998, 1072a, p. 373.
26. Aristotle, *The Metaphysics,* 1998, 1072a, p. 373.
27. Aristotle, *The Metaphysics* 1998, 1072b, p. 374.
28. Cf. Armstrong, *An Introduction to Ancient Philosophy,* 1947, pp. 88-9.
29. Aristotle, *The Metaphysics,*1998, 1072b, p. 374
30. Aristotle, *The Metaphysics,* 1998, 983a, 6-9, p. 10; Barnes 1995, pp. 102-3.
31. Aristotle, *Magna Moralia* 1208b, 27-30.
32. 35-Cf. Gerson, *God and Greek Philosophy,* 1991, pp. 132-33.
33. Aristotle, *The Metaphysics,* 1998, 1074a, pp. 379-80; Cf. Armstrong, 1947, p. 90.
34. Cf. Ziai, H. 'Mulla Sadra:His life and works', in Nasr and Leaman, ed, *History of Islamic Philosophy,* 1996, pp. 635-42; Cooper, Mulla Sadra Shirazi." In: E. Craig, ed. *The Routledge Encyclopaedia of Philosophy,* 1998, pp. 595-99. The best general study on him is still Rahman, *The Philosophy of Mulla Sadra,* 1975.
35. His magnum opus. See Rahman pp. 744-47.
36. Mulla Sadra, *al-Hikma al-muta'aliya fi l-asfar al-'aqliyya al-arba'a.* 3rd ed. Beirut: Dar ihya' al-turath al-'arabi, vol 6, 1981, pp. 12-14.
37. Mulla Sadra, *al-Hikma al-muta'aliya fi l-asfar al-'aqliyya al-arba'a.* 3rd ed. Beirut: Dar ihya' al-turath al-'arabi, vol 6 1981, pp. 14.
38. Cf. Rahman 1975, pp. 125-38.
39. Mulla Sadra, *al-Hikma al-muta'aliya fi l-asfar al-'aqliyya al-arba'a.* 3rd ed. Beirut: Dar ihya' al-turath al-'arabi, vol 61981, pp. 14-15.
40. Mulla Sadra, *al-Hikma al-muta'aliya fi l-asfar al-'aqliyya al-arba'a.* 3rd ed. Beirut: Dar ihya' al-turath al-'arabi, vol 6 1981, pp. 23-24.
41. Mulla Sadra, *al-Hikma al-muta'aliya fi l-asfar al-'aqliyya al-arba'a.* 3rd ed. Beirut: Dar ihya' al-turath al-'arabi, vol 61981, p. 24.
42. Mulla Sadra, *al-Hikma al-muta'aliya fi l-asfar al-'aqliyya al-arba'a.* 3rd ed. Beirut: Dar ihya' al-turath al-'arabi, vol 6 1981, p 24.
43. Mulla Sadra, *al-Hikma al-muta'aliya fi l-asfar al-'aqliyya al-arba'a.* 3rd ed. Beirut: Dar ihya' al-turath al-'arabi, vol 6 1981, p. 118.

44. Mulla Sadra, *al-Hikma al-muta'aliya fi l-asfar al-'aqliyya al-arba'a*. 3rd ed. Beirut: Dar ihya' al-turath al-'arabi, vol 6 1981, p. 118.
45. Mulla Sadra, *al-Hikma al-muta'aliya fi l-asfar al-'aqliyya al-arba'a*. 3rd ed. Beirut: Dar ihya' al-turath al-'arabi, vol 6,1981, p. 118.
46. Mulla Sadra, *al-Hikma al-muta'aliya fi l-asfar al-'aqliyya al-arba'a*. 3rd ed. Beirut: Dar ihya' al-turath al-'arabi, vol 6,1981, p. 120.
47. Amuli, *Sharh-I Asfar- Arba'a*,1996, p.339.
48. Mulla Sadra, *al-Mabda' wa l-Ma'ad*, 1967, p. 38-9; Cf. Mulla Sadra 1981, pp. 125-49.
49. Mulla Sadra, *al-Mabda' wa l-Ma'ad*, 1967, p. 39; Mulla Sadra 1981, pp. 167-74.
50. Misbah Yazdi, *Philosophical Instruction*, 1999, p. 531.
51. Cf. Mulla Sadra, *Asfar*, 1981, pp. 180 ff.
52. Mulla Sadra, *al-Mabda' wa l-Ma'ad*, 1976, p. 90.
53. Mulla Sadra, *al-Mabda' wa l-Ma'ad*, 1976, p. 121; Cf. Mulla Sadra 1981, pp. 110-18.
54. Mulla Sadra, *Asfar*, 1981, p. 413.
55. Cf. Mulla Sadra, *Asfar*, 1981, pp. 334ff; Misbah-i Yazdi 1999, pp. 535-36.
56. Mulla Sadra, Asfar, 1981, pp. 421-24.
57. Mulla Sadra,Asfar, 1981, p. 422-423.
58. Mulla Sadra, Asfar, 1981, pp. 13-14.
59. Mulla Sadra, Asfar, 1981, p. 281.
60. Mulla Sadra, *al-Shawahid al-Rububiyya*, 1967, p. 145.
61. Mulla Sadra, *al-Shawahid al-Rububiyya*, 1967, p. 147.

Rumi and Mulla Sadra on Theoretical and Practical Intellect

Introduction:

In contemporary Western languages the essential difference between intellect (*intellectus*) and reason (*ratio*) that one finds in Christian philosophy of the Middle Ages is generally forgotten, and the word intellect is used for all practical purposes as a synonym for reason. (On the distinction between intellect and reason, see Nasr, *"Knowledge and the Sacred"*, chapter 1 and 4). In Islamic languages a single word, *'aql*, is used to indicate both reason and intellect, but the difference between the two as well as their interrelationship and the dependence of reason upon the intellect is always reserved in mind. Al *'aql* in Arabic language is from the root *'ql*, which means to bind. It means it is the faculty that binds man to the Truth, to God, to his Source and Beginning. *'Aql* is also used to indicate both reason and intelligence.

In Islamic thought, practical intellect involves the use of reason in any decision about how to act. This contrasts with theoretical intellect (often called speculative intellect), which refers to the use of reason in deciding what to believe. For example: scientists use practical reason to decide how to build a telescope, but theoretical intellect to decide which of two theories of light and optics is the best.

Rumi's Points of view on intellect:

Rumi (1207-1273), the great 13th Persian *Arif*/sage, uses approximately 34 terms for Intellect in his masterpiece *Mathnawi*. They may be categorised into three main types:

1- Meta-theoretical and Practical intellect, which are also known as Universal Intellect and First intellect. God generates the First intellect. The Universal intellect/ *'Aql kull* is the first creation of God, through which He then creates the universe.
2- Theoretical intellect, which is used to distinguish between truth and untruth, truth and falsehood, and right and wrong. Theoretical intellect comprises faithful intellect (*'Aql-Imani*), perfect intellect (*'Aql kamil*), honourable intellect (*'Aql Sharif*) and Divine Intellect (*'Aql Rabani*).

According to Rumi, the origin of intellect is Universal Intellect *'Aql Kull*.[1]

Faithful intellect is based on faith and contributes importantly to the search for knowledge and perfection.[2] It has a deep and strong connection with the spiritual world.

'Aql Kamil/perfect intellect[3] is engaged in seeing truth and looking towards the Absolute Truth and the Creator of the Universal Intellect. It is in use when one is receiving knowledge from the Absolute Wise / *'Alim*.

The honourable intellect/ *'Aql Sharif*[4] is that which has capacity to find and see the truth. *Nafs Amarih*/ carnal soul and physical senses are its opposites. They try to stop it from accessing truth. This intellect is *Nur-i Latif*/ fine light.

Another term Rumi used, which was very close to the *'Aql Sharif*, was *'Aql Jalil*/the glorious-great intellect[5] This is the intellect that travels towards God (*Sayr-i Ila Allah*) and allows one to understand secrets of the *Haqq*.

The Divine Intellect /*Aql Rabani* is a form of intellect that never sees anything without seeing God therein. The divine intellect is the intellect of the mystic who has reached union with God and who has submerged his intellect in the universal intellect and has therefore become divine.

The divine intellect is capable of understanding and discovering the realities of the material/physical world and the Divine/metaphysical world, and comprehends existence as a whole.

The process of the transformation and perfection of the partial intellect into the divine intellect is by the revolution, changes and transformations that occur in the mystics' understanding and spiritual needs. The key requirement for achieving this transformation is to sever one's ties and attachments to the world.[6]

> 3- Practical intellect serves to distinguish between Good and evil. The components of practical intellect are material reason, resurrection intellect, partial reason, popular reason, and brief reason.

Discursive reason *'Aql Ma'ash*[7] pays attention only to the material world and to gaining benefit through material means. *'Aql Ma'ash* is superseded by *'Aql Ma'ad*.[8]

By contrast with material reason, the resurrection intellect/*'Aql Ma'ad*[9] attends closely to God in all acts and manners in personal and social life. This intellect is connected to the spiritual world and its judgments are made according to divine values. The resurrection intellect is reserved for those who have escaped from the bondage of the carnal or discursive reason/ *'Aql Ma'ash*.[10]

The partial intellect *'Aql Jozei*[11] is a type of reason that thinks only of the material life. Partial reason can accomplish the control of the *Nafs-Amarih*, with the clear example in the story "the Caliph, the Arab of the Desert and his wife in book one of Rumi's Mathnawi" of the *'Aql/* intellect being taken in by *Nafs/*soul and being infected with worldliness.[12]

The popular reason/*'Aql 'Awam*[13] is reason that can't understand transcendent and Divine's values.

The brief reason /*Aql Mokhtasar*[14] is reason that does not distinguished between pure and tainted or impure acts.

According to Rumi everyone has reason, which, upon finding a perfect man, may help him to transcend from partial reason to Universal intellect.

Mulla Sadra's views on intellect:

According to Mulla Sadra (1571-1641), the great 17th century Iranian Muslim philosopher, *Nafs-e Natiqeh* (rational soul) is the distinguishing factor between mankind and animals. This faculty can understand *Kolyyat/* universals and *Jozeiyat/*partials and is also *Motosarif/*possessing meanings and forms. This faculty has two sub-faculties/*quweh,* which are called the Theoretical Intellect and the Practical intellect. These forms of intellect refer to mankind's potential to learn knowledge from his superior which is the "world of intellects"/ *'Alam al-'uqul* or the Active intellect, and his ability to manage that which is inferior/*Madun* to it. Theoretical intellect understands *Tasawurat*/ideas and *Tasdiqat*/judgments and is able to identify truth and falseness, while Practical intellect comprehends mankind's acts and manners and identifies them as positive or negative, good or bad. There are four types of theoretical and practical intellect, based on perfection.[15]

Theoretical Intellect:

Theoretical intellect ascends from "material reason" *('aql hayuluni),* "habitual intellect" *('aql bi al-malakeh),* and "intellect in act" *('aql bi al-fi'l)* to the "acquired intellect" *('aql bi al mustafad).* The human being possesses intelligence in virtuality. The four divisions of the theoretical intellect are as follows:

The first division is called material or potential intellect / *bil-quwah,* due to its similarity to *hayula,* or prime matter. Material or potential intellect corresponds with unintelligibility and potentiality in relation to all forms.

The second division manifests itself as the soul grows in knowledge and the first intelligible forms are placed in the soul from the above. In this stage, man ascends to the level of the habitual intellect/ *al-'aql bil-malikah,* which he is able to understand self-evident concepts (*tasawwurat*) and judgments (*tasdiqat*). This progression grows from the fact that the knowledge of self-evident matters (*badihiyat*) precedes the knowledge of speculative matters (*nazariyyeh*).

Further on, as the intellect becomes fully actualised in the mind, man reaches the third division of actual intellect / *bil-f'il,* which understands speculative matters through the mediation of self-evident concepts and judgments. Once this process is completed, man reaches the fourth stage of acquired intellect / *mustafad,* which is the intellect that partakes of all self-evident and speculative intelligible [knowledge?] corresponding to the realities of the higher and lower realms of existence by virtue of having all of them present before it and its actual consciousness of them having been achieved. Thus acquired intellect corresponds with a "knowledge world" similar to the external world.

Finally above these stages stands the Active Intellect al-*'aql-al-Fa'al.*, which is Divine, and illuminates the mind through the act of knowledge.[16]

Practical intellect:

Practical intellect may be divided into the following:

Firstly, the polishing/refinement of apparent/outer part, secondly, polishing the inner part, thirdly, illuminating the heart, and finally the annihilation of the soul from its essence.[17]

The first stage involves practicing the orders of divine messengers. This includes praying, fasting, avoiding wine, abstaining from free sex, and refraining from gambling, stealing, murder, etc.

The second stage involves removing oneself completely from any immoral activity which could transfer the light heart into the dark heart. These include lying, accusation, defamation, backbiting, pride, arrogance, anger, selfishness etc.

"عقلها دیدم بسان نورها

لیک پنهان گشته در نار هوی

چشم عقل ار چند باشد عین نور

خاک شهوت سازدش در گور کور

چشم عقل ار چند باشد نور پاک

کور می گردد چو دل بندد به خاک"[i] [18]

"I have seen intellects the like of lights
But they are hidden by the fire of lust
The eye of intellect although like light
Blind it is turned in the grave by the soil of lust
The eye of intellect although pure light
Blind it is turned when it falls for soil"

"عقل و شهوت ضد یکدیگر بود

چون کلید و قفل بر یک دیگر بود

عقل تو خوابید چون شهوت بخاست

زان که شهوت ضد عقل است و سخاست

شهوتت بر خاست عقل کرد خواب

عقل خواب آلود، کی باشد صواب

شهوت از خاک است و عقل از کردگار

کردگار و خاک را با هم چه کار"[i] [19]

"Countering each other intellect and lust
As luck and key on one door they are
Once lust awoke your intellect slept
As countering intellect and generosity is lust.
Your lust awoke and your intellect slept
When is a drowsy intellect right
Lust is from soil and from the creator is the intellect
What are the creator and soil to one other"

The third stage corresponds with the illuminating of the heart by the light of "knowledge forms" (*suwar-al-ilmiyyah*) and praiseworthy attributes. The fourth stage—the annihilation of the soul from its essence—can only be achieved through full attention to God and His holy presence.[20]

According to Mulla Sadra's transcendent philosophy, which is based on the "principality of Being" (*asalat wujud*) each act of knowledge involves the being of the knower. And the hierarchy of the faculties of knowledge correspond to the hierarchy of existence. Intellect is in its essence a Divine light and practical intellect is based on Theoretical intellect which in essence is the illuminative intellect.

"نفس چون کامل شد از علم و عمل

عقده گیتی بر او گردید حل

هر دو قوت رو به علیین نهند

جملگی جسم و روان را جان دهند"[iii] [21]

"Once the soul is perfected from knowledge and act
Solved for it is the problem of the world
Both attributes are eminent
As they both give life to the body and soul"

Conclusion:

Intellect makes no mistake. It is that other thing that makes mistakes.[22]

Purification of the soul/heart from its material defilement, *Tajaruud*/catharsis, is of utmost importance for both Rumi and Mulla Sadra, for having pure theoretical and practical intellect. Both philosophers also emphasised that only by connecting to the universal intellect can man's intellect guide him to the truth and to good acts/*'Amal hasan*.

Both thinkers believe that the purification of the intellect occurs by way of spiritual love. And *'Aql*/intellect and *Jan/Ruh*/spirit are used by both to denote the Divine Essence under different aspects.

In Islamic thought, a millennium of discussion on the relations between demonstration/*burhan* related to the faculty of intellect, mysticism/*'Irfan* related to the faculty of the heart/intellect associated with inner intuition and illumination, and Qur'an or revelation related to the prophetic function reaches its peak in the synthesis of Mulla Sadra's transcendent philosophy.

Note. Abbreviations: R: Rumi, M: Mathnawi, B: Book, V: verse.

References:

Nasr, Seyyed Hossein. *Knowledge and the Sacred*. New York, 1981.
Nasr, Seyyed Hossein. *Islamic Philosophy from its Origin to the Present*, chapter 6, New York, 2006.
Mulla Sadra. *Al-Shawahid al-rububiyyah*.Tehran, 1987.
Mulla Sadra. *Mathnawi*. edited by Fayzi, Mustafa, Qum, 1376.
Mulla Sadra. *Fi Itahad-I al-'aqil wa al-m'qul*, in *Majmieh Rasael Falsafi-I Sadr al-Mot'alehin*. edited by Naji Isfahani, Hamid. Tehran, 1996.
Rumi, J. *Mathnawi*. edited by Estelami, Mohammad, Tehran, 1379.

- *Fihi ma Fih*. edited, Foruzanfar, Badi'al Zaman,Tehran, 1983.

Safavi, Seyed G. *The Structure of Rumi's Mathnawi*. London, 2006.

- *The structure of the third book of Rumi's Mathnai as a whole*, in Transcendent Philosophy Journal, vol.9, 2008. London.
- *Rumi's Thought*. Tehran 2003,
- *Rumi Teachings*. Philadelphia, 2008.
- *Perception according to Mulla Sadra*. Tehran, 2002.

Shams-Tabrizi. *Me & Rumi*. translated by Chittick, William, Kentucky, 2004.
Shams-Tabrizi. *Maqalat Sham-Tabrizi*. edited by Movahhed.Mohammad.Ali, Tehran, 1369.
Tabataba'i, Allamah, Sayyid Muhammad Husayn. *Bidayat al-Hikmah*, traaslated to English by Qara'i, Sayyid Ali Quli. London, 2003.

- *Nihayat al-Hikmah*. Tehran, 1370 Sh./1991.
- *Usul Falsafeh wa Rawish Realism*.commentary by Mutahhari, Murtaza, Qum, 1364 Sh./1985.

Endnotes:

1. See Rumi, Mathnawi, book 1, verses 1906-1910.
2. R.M.B4, V1987, 1983-1992.
3. R.M.B5,V739.
4. R.M.B2.V 3514 and 3514-3520.
5. R.M.B1, V 3325.
6. See Discourse five to eight in *The structure of the third book of Rumi's Mathnawi as a whole*, Safavi, Seyed G. in *Transcendent Philosophy Journal*, vol. 9, 2008. London.

7. R.M.B1.V. 1065.
8. See Safavi, *The Structure of Rumi's Mathnawi*, Discourse four and eight, 2006.
9. R.M.B1, V.14.
10. See Safavi, *The Structure of Rumi's Mathnawi*, Discourse four and eight.
11. R.M.B1, V 2881, 3503, B3, V.15590, 3585, B4, V.1247, 3031, B5, 460-468.
12. See Discourse one to four in *"The structure and Hermeneutics of the third book of Rumi's Mathnawi as a whole"*, Safavi, Seyed G, Transcendent Philosophy Journal, vol. 9, 2008, p5-34.
13. R.M.B4, V. 3287 and 3288-3300.
14. R.M.B4, V. 2174, 2170-2178.
15. Mulla Sadra, *Ishraq 8, Mashhad* 3 in *al-Shawahid al-rububiyyah*. Mulla Sadra, *Mathnawi*,.Mulla Sadra, *Fi Itahad al-'aqil wa al-m'aqul*, in *Majmieh Rasael Falsafi-I Sadr al-Mut'alehin*.
16. See Mulla Sadra, *Ishraq 9-12, Mashhad3* in *Shawahi al robobyyeh* and Allameh M.H. Tabatabaei, the elements of Islamic Metaphysics, chapter 7 and chapter 6, part 11 in *Nihayat al hikmat*, Nasr, Islamic Philosophy from its Origin to the Present, Chapter 6.
17. See Mulla Sadra, *Ishraq13, Mashhad 3* in *Shawahi al robobyyeh*.
18. Mulla Sadra, Mathnawi, p.162.
19. Mulla Sadra, Mathnawi, p.163.
20. See Mulla Sadra, *Shawahi al rububeyyeh, Ishraq* 13.
21. Mulla Sadra, Mathnawi, p165.
22. See Chittick, Me and Rumi, The Autobiography of Shams-I Tabrizi, p.22, see also Chittick's point of view on intellect according to Rumi in p 381.

Mulla Sadra and Descartes On the Soul: A Philosophical Comparison

Introduction

The question of "the soul" is amongst the most complex philosophical topics in the history of philosophy, and in human thought itself. For his part, Averroes (1126-1198) considered it impossible to provide a definition for the soul. Mulla Sadra (1572-1640), the Muslim Iranian philosopher who founded *al-Hikmah al-Muta'aliyah* (Transcendent Philosophy), and René Descartes (1596-1650), the French thinker who is often considered to have founded modern western philosophy, both established philosophical systems that have had significant consequences. It is instructive to consider a comparative analysis of the opinions of these two philosophers in regards to the important topic of the soul.

This chapter examines the philosophical views of Mulla Sadra and Descartes on the soul. The comparison is divided into five main segments, as follows:

1. An Exposition of Mulla Sadra's Discussion of the Soul
2. An Exposition of Descartes' Discussion of the Soul
3. Similarities and Differences Between the Two
4. Strengths of Mulla Sadra's Theory
5. Critiques of Descartes' Theory

The foundation of Mulla Sadra's theory is "the corporeality of contingency and the spirituality of subsistence in relation to the soul." The foundation of Descartes' theory is "the real distinction between the substance of the soul and the body." Mulla Sadra's theory includes a philosophical proof for physical resurrection, whereas Descartes' dualism led to the collapse of his philosophical system.

The Soul According to Mulla Sadra

Besides his philosophical views on the soul, Mulla Sadra has also examined the soul from the perspective offered in the Holy Qur'an, in theology, and in prophetic narrations. The term "philosophical" in the subheading of this section signifies that this article only deals with Mulla Sadra's philosophical arguments, which relate to the themes also covered by Descartes.

According to many philosophers, the soul is a substance that is essentially independent from the body. For it to act requires matter; thus is attached to, and governs, bodies. In Aristotle's opinion, "the soul is the first natural, organized body potentially possessing life."[1] In contrast to other philosophers who consider the human soul to be static, Mulla Sadra considers it to be gradational.

Mulla Sadra's theory of the soul is important and innovative in the way it describes the soul. Famously, he says, "the soul is corporeal in its origination but spiritual in its subsistence,"[2] because the human soul, to originate and be manifest, requires matter, and uses the potentialities of the body. The soul is considered to be an organ of the body; this is the reason for Mulla Sadra's argument that the soul does not require an existence separate from that of the body. Mulla Sadra uses the principle of "transubstantial motion" (which is amongst his important philosophical innovations) to prove that it is possible for a material phenomenon, that has the potential to become abstract, to slowly gain an immaterial form—with the help of transubstantial motion. Finally, he concludes that the matter of the soul, is the same as the matter of the body, and that the soul is a physical reality which desires to ascend to the spiritual world (*malakut*).

The soul passes through the following stages in its journey towards perfection: in the foetal period, the soul is a vegetative state. At birth, the soul is animal in actuality, and human in potentiality. Through a life of thinking and contemplation, it is at around the age of forty that (the soul) becomes human in actuality. The soul is a unified essence, and has both the faculty of audition and that of vision. Besides being capable of thought it has a sensual faculty. Mulla Sadra considers the evolutionary journey of the soul to be harmonious with, and to occur alongside, the process of general universal motion. This motion begins with matter, proceeds through a stage in which it transcends matter, and ultimately ends at the most abstract stage.

In the following books Mulla Sadra deals with different topics related to the soul: *'Arshiyyah, Masha'ir, Mabda' wa Ma'ad, Shawahid al-Robubiyyah, Asfar* and *Hashiyeh bar Hikmat al-Ishraq-e Suhrewardi*. Relevant topics include how the soul is made, the relation between the soul and the body, the substance of the soul, the degrees of the soul, the evolutionary journey of the soul, the immateriality of the soul, and the subsistence of the soul.

First Principle: The Soul Is Gradational

The human soul, from the beginning of its creation to its telos, has various ranks; that is, it passes through different existential stages. As such, the soul is not static; rather, it is dynamic, alive and gradational. In its initial attachment to the body, the soul is referred to as a "corporeal substance"; after that, it gains in power from stage to stage, and is transformed into the different forms of its creation until it no longer needs the body and can subsist on its own. After leaving the body, the soul is separate from the material world, and journeys towards the eternal world, to return to its Lord. On the basis of this journey and this principle, "the soul is corporeal in its origination but spiritual in its subsistence."[3] On this basis, when it is first manifested in the material world, it is a physical power; after that it transforms into the sensual soul, and, by passing through the different degrees of sensuality, it reaches a stage where it is capable of creating different forms within its essence. In this latter stage it is referred to as '*Mofakkirah*,' meaning it has the ability to think. After this, the soul retains what it discovers within itself, and this ability—the ability to remember—is referred to as "*dhakirah*." By ascending beyond this stage, the soul reaches the rank of intellection, at which point it comprehends the universalities of the world. After this it reaches the rank of the "practical intellect" (*'aql al-'amali*), and then the rank of "speculative intellect" (*'aql al-nadhari*). The ranks of the speculative intellect are, "the intellect of potentiality," (*'aql bi al-quwwah*), the "intellect of actuality" (*'aql bi al-fi'l*), and the "active intellect" (*'aql fa'al*). The body and the soul constantly transform until they reach their ultimate state and supreme origin[4].

Second Principle: The Actualization of the Active Intellect in the Human Soul

The active intellect has two existences, "non-relational" and "relational." The relational existence of the active intellect is its existence *within* the human essence, and *for* the human being. Thus, the perfection and completion of the human being is the existence of the active intellect in her or him; it is the connection and union he or she has with the active intellect. This theory predicates the existence of the active intellect on the existence of the soul, and considers the active intellect to be the soul's last stage of perfection. In the beginning of creation and in the initial periods of its origination, the soul moves towards the perfection of the natural physical body and the origin of some of the vegetative and animal acts. In this stage, it is a potential thing. Afterwards, by beginning to acquire power over realities, knowledge and wisdom, the soul can categorize and organize issues, and can order policies related to the laws of life. Thus it becomes an intellectual being and attains the rank of an "intellect of actuality." On its path from potentiality to actuality, the soul is in need of the aid and attention of a being superior to itself; and, as it does not possess an innate intellect or intellectual perfection, it is in need of another being which possesses both. There is an end to this chain of need; the end is divine light that is connected to a being named "the active intellect." And this intellect is perfect, actual, and active; it governs the soul, it is devoid of imperfection and lack, and it leads the soul from potentiality to actuality. As such, the soul, by uniting with this actual perfect being, attains "actual intellect," and understands everything.[5]

Third Principle: The External and Internal Faculties of the Soul

In addition to the five external faculties, the soul has five internal faculties that are the principles of the external faculties. The external faculties become inactive as a result of unconsciousness and death; however, the internal faculties do not become inactive, for the soul of the human being has collective unity, which is the ray of the light of "the true unity of reality."

Fourth Principle: The Soul and the Body Are Not Two Things

Before Mulla Sadra, philosophers were of the opinion that the soul is an addition to the body. This theory supplements the notion that the body and the soul are two things; in this view, the relationship between the soul and the body is like that of an entity controlling another entity. However, in Mulla Sadra's opinion the soul and the body are not two separate things. Initially, the soul is referred to as the soul for it is exactly like the essence of its substance, and it is not dependent on anything else (i.e., it is not separate from the body, nor is it a later addition to the body). Rather, initially the soul is considered to be one stage among the stages of the body. Once the soul is transformed and gains perfection by intellection and knowledge, it separates from the body. Thus, it is only when the soul becomes pure intellect, independent in its own essence, that it leaves the body and becomes self-subsistent, and no longer in need of the body.[6]

Fifth Principle: Human Beings Initially Fall Under a Single Definition of Species, But in the Second Stage They Have Different Essences

Human beings are united in one species. The definition of the species refers to the proximate genus (*Jins qarib*) and the proximate difference (*Fasl-e qarib*); these terms refer to bodily matter and the form of the soul. However, human souls in the initial stage move towards a change of essence, and become different species falling under four genera. In the beginning of existence and the initial stage of actuality, souls are forms of perfection for the sensible material body. At the same time they are also spiritual matter. If accompanied by the aid of an intellective form, this matter moves from a stage of potentiality to that of actuality. If, however, the soul is accompanied by a delusional, satanic, brutal and bestial form, it will, on the day of resurrection, be resurrected in that form. This resurrection occurs in the other world—otherwise it would be transmigration, and not resurrection. Transmigration is impossible, whereas bodily resurrection is real, and can neither be escaped nor avoided. In the end the human being will be transformed into the form of an angel, into Satan, or into a four-legged or brutal animal. If knowledge and God-consciousness (*taqwa*) dominate the human soul, it will appear as an angel, but if deceit, trickery and compounded ignorance overcome the soul, it becomes Satan. If the effects of lust dominate the soul, it will turn into a four-legged animal. If it is dominated by anger, it becomes a brutal beast. As such, the actuality of each thing is based on its form[7] and not its matter. In the other world the matter of the human being (ie., skin-colour or race) is of no importance; rather, the foundation of resurrection is the form and actuality of the human being. As such, the human being is resurrected based on the moralities and values that dominate its soul.[8]

Sixth Principle: The Transformation of the Soul Based on Transubstantial Motion

The transformation of the stages of the soul, according to the theory of transubstantial motion, is one of Mulla Sadra's important innovations. By criticising the opinions of previous philosophers concerning the static nature of the soul, as he does in the book *Arshiyah*, he clarifies and answers the problems posed by earlier thinkers. For instance, some say that it is one of the certainties of philosophy that one object cannot, at the same time, be the form of one object and the substance of the form of another, unless the form is removed, and afterwards the substance becomes something else. Based on this, some argue, it cannot be said that the essence of the human soul becomes manifest in the form of an internal soul. But in answer to them Mulla Sadra says, such an argument is based on the presupposition that in the world only one state of being occurs, or else the object under discussion is abstract and unchangeable. However, the soul, due to its dependence upon the body, is capable of becoming powerful and, at the same time, being the material form of this world. For it is a substance for the form of the other world; this very soul is capable of becoming like the lowest form of animals in the material world through bad deeds, and yet it can also be a substance prepared to accept the highest form of the other world. Thus, although the corporeal form is in actuality the form of the body, it can potentially become a substance for the intellectual form.

Mulla Sadra proves that the universal natures all undergo transubstantial motion and, in this world, transform from one form to another. Thus it is not necessary to accept the opinion of past philosophers, who, since they considered bodies and essences to be static, did not discover transubstantial motion.

The human soul undergoes a revolution sooner than other beings. In general, the body, the soul and the intellect proceed through different natural stages. In the beginning of creation the soul possesses the greatest degree of sensuality, and possesses only the beginning of the spiritual world. The soul is "the great gate of Allah," for with its aid one can reach the world of angels; also, however, every characteristic of hell can be seen within it. The soul is a barrier between this world and the other world, for it is both the form of the forces of this world and also the material of all the forms of the other world. The soul "is the meeting place of corporeality and spirituality." The soul, as the ultimate form of different spiritualties and bodies, is in its first stage of the bodily and spiritual realities, and is not solely of the body.[9]

The Seventh Principle: Combining the Contingency and the Subsistence of the Soul

Khawjah Nisar al-DinTusi puts forward the following criticism: how is possible to combine the contingency of the soul and its subsistence? For whatever proof is presented for contingency will also act as a proof for the transiency of the soul; and whichever proof is set forth for the subsistence of the soul is also a proof for its eternality—and, as such, is a negation of its contingency.

Mulla Sadra argues that the soul, in contrast to pure abstracts and to pure bodies, is not limited to one world, but rather possesses different modalities of being. On the one hand, it possesses an abstract and intellectual modality. On the other, it exists in the natural world, and on the basis of this it is contingent. The contingency of this specific modality of the modalities of the world is based on the condition of the body. The soul enters the abstract world in its evolutionary journey; by entering the abstract world—that is, through this transformation—it dies in the natural world and is resurrected in the abstract world. It is evident that, in this stage of the soul's being, there is no need for the body, nor for material conditions. Thus, the annihilation of the body does not in any way harm the intellect, but rather results in the end of the state of attachment and the natural being of the soul. The state of attachment is transient and ceases after the annihilation of the body. However, besides this state, the soul acquires an abstract being and, because of that state, is subsistent[10].

Descartes' Theory:

Descartes' theory in regards to the soul has come to be known as Cartesian dualism, for he believed in a substantial distinction between the soul and the body. The following text considers Descartes' theory in regards to the "distinction of soul and body," "spiritual substance," and the eternality of the soul.

The Distinction Between the Soul and the Body

According to Descartes' theory, the soul is not material, for its substance is thought; further, it does not possess the material characteristics of the body. In the introduction to the *Meditations*, Descartes says that the distinction between the body and the soul is based on the reducibility of the body, and the irreducibility of the soul. That is, the body must be considered a reducible form, whereas the soul must be considered irreducible (in the sense that one cannot imagine half of the soul). The soul and the body are two distinct entities; no two entities could be more distinct from one another. By His power, God has created the substance of the soul and that of the body to be entirely distinct.[11]

Descartes considers "thought" to be the essential characteristic of the soul, and extension to be the essential characteristic of the body.[12] He says that the presence of the soul in the body is not analogous to the presence of a captain in the ship; rather, the soul is united with the whole of the body. The soul, at the same time, is distinct from the body in action, although it is united with it.[13] My body, as I clearly see it, is a substance; however, it is a material substance, just as my spirit is a thinking substance. Thus, that which is referred to as "I" has two distinct parts: the "body," or the machine that works, and the "soul," or the engineer that thinks.[14]

In principle 8 of *the principles of philosophy* Descartes writes:

In this way we discover the distinction between soul and body, or between a thinking thing and physical thing.

This is the best way to discover the nature of the mind and its distinction from the body. Since we are supposing that everything which is distinct from us is non-existent, if we examine what we are we see that no extension shape or local motion, or anything similar which should be attributed to the body pertains or our nature apart from thought alone. Therefore, thought is known prior to and more certainly than anything physical because we have already perceived our thought while we are still doubting other things.

The Substance of the Soul and Its Existence Independent From the Body

The foundation of Descartes' argument for the abstract quality of the soul is "cogito ergo sum." In the second meditation, Descartes aims to attain truth through the application of methodical doubt. He comes to reason that, in the process of doubt, he can come to doubt everything except himself. He says that his "I" cannot be doubted, for it is that which is doubting in the first place, and that even the doubts caused by the deceitful Satan cannot make his "I" itself seem doubtful. For if he has been deceived, he must *be*, and as such, he *is*. With this reasoning, Descartes aims to prove the existence of the thinking self. Descartes argues that actions such as eating and movement belong to the body and not to the "I," whereas thinking belongs to the 'I' and cannot be removed from it. He further argues that the perception of the wax (body), not by the senses or imagination, but by the intellect alone, is evidence for the existence of the soul as a substance independent from the body, for the wax has been perceived without the aid of the physical senses.[15]

The Immortality and Subsistence of the Soul

Descartes is of the opinion that the soul is immortal and subsistent. However, like Plato, he does not consider the immortality of the soul to be the result of the soul's simplicity; rather, he considers the soul to be subsistent because it is a substance. He is of the opinion that all substances, be they physical or spiritual, are subsistent.

Commonalities and Differences Between Mulla Sadra and Descartes

This section addresses similarities and differences between the two philosophers' accounts.

The Commonalities Between Descartes and Mulla Sadra

Mulla Sadra and Descartes are in agreement with regard to a number of important philosophical principles concerning the soul, although they use different arguments to prove these principles. These are: 1. The soul as substance; 2. The soul as abstract and spiritual; 3. The eternality of the soul; 4. The soul's union with, and distinction from, the body.

The Differences Between Descartes and Mulla Sadra

The difference between Descartes' and Mulla Sadra's accounts of the soul are: 1. Descartes considers the soul to be "spirituality of contingency and spirituality of subsistence," whereas Mulla Sadra characterizes the soul as "corporeality of contingency and spirituality of subsistence." 2. Descartes considers the soul to be static, whereas Mulla Sadra considers it to be dynamic. 3. Descartes considers the soul to have only one stage, whereas Mulla Sadra considers it to be gradational: "the soul before nature," "the soul in nature," and "the soul after leaving matter." 4. Their arguments for proving the eternality of the soul differ. Descartes considers the soul to be eternal because it is a substance; even material substances are eternal in his philosophy. However, Mulla Sadra considers the eternality of the soul to be due to the abstractness of the soul, and its relation to the world of intellects. As the absolute abstraction of contingent being, it is dependent on absolute, simple, abstract existence 5. According to Descartes, the soul and the body are two discrete entities; one is added to the other. In Mulla Sadra's opinion this is not the case; rather, the soul is referred to as such because it is exactly like the essence of its substance and it is not an addition to anything. In the beginning the soul is considered to be one of the stages of the body, and afterwards it gains perfection, acquires wisdom and knowledge, and becomes abstract. 6. Descartes considers the relation between the body and the soul through epiphysis; this is the major weakness of his philosophical system. For his part, Mulla Sadra explains the relation between the body and the soul through "the gradational nature of existence," "the gradations of the soul," and "transubstantial motion."

The Distinct Strength of Mulla Sadra's Theory of the Soul

Based on the theory of "the corporeality of contingency and the spirituality of subsistence" of the soul, Mulla Sadra has proven bodily resurrection using a philosophical instead of a theological method. In Mulla Sadra's philosophical system, the soul arises from the material foundation and, through transubstantial motion, passes through the stages of abstractness, one after the other, and becomes more complete. At the time of natural death, the soul is perfect, and has no need for the body. After the separation of the soul from the body, the faculty of imagination (which is abstract) is strengthened, and creates the metaphorical body; however, this does not hinder the reality of the material or the after-life body. This is because, for the human being, the body is matter. Matter here is considered in terms of genus; that is, not simply in terms of the physical. Matter in this sense also refers, for example, to bodies of light; as such, the term "body" can also be applied to the metaphorical body. The philosophical principles of Mulla Sadra's proof for bodily resurrection are: the "supreme reality of existence," the "reality of particularity and existence," the "gradation of being," "transubstantial motion," and "abstractness of imagination." However, Descartes' philosophy is incapable of offering rational proof for bodily resurrection.

Descartes' Mechanical Philosophy

Descartes' philosophy cannot adequately explain the relation between the body and the soul, because his is a mechanical and plurality-oriented philosophy. This account ignores the dynamism present in the natural world (on the basis of transubstantial motion), and does not acknowledge the existential unity of being. For instance, the human being itself possesses multiplicity. Missing this point, however, Descartes explains the relationship between substances and being by positing the direct, mechanic role of God. In general, Descartes' philosophy is a "static" philosophy, whereas the philosophies of Mulla Sadra, Leibniz and Hegel are "dynamic" systems of philosophy.

The Relation of the Body and the Soul

The statement that the relation between the body and the soul is accidental, and that there is no necessary relation between the two, is false. Like Aristotle, Descartes described the soul as the "first perfection" of the instrumental natural body. It is impossible for such a composition to arise from two things that have no causal relation. The relation between soul and body is a necessary relation. Such a relation is not like the coincidence of opposites, and it is not like the relation of two effects of one cause that have no direct relation with each other. Also, the relation of the body and the soul is not the relation of the absolute cause with its effect; rather, it is the relation of two entities that are necessary for each other: each, from a distinct aspect, requires the other, and they are dependent on each other in being. The body requires a connection to the soul in order to be actualised. And, although the soul does not require the body in terms of reality and intellectual being, it does need a capable body for generation; thus, the soul comes to exist in the body and belongs to it.[16] This is why Mulla Sadra considers the soul to be material and not abstract in its early manifestation in the body (the corporeality of contingency and the spirituality of subsistence). This explains the relation between a material and an abstract entity.

Cartesian Dualism

Descartes' metaphor of machine (body) and engineer (soul) is a dualistic philosophical notion, which separates the world into two separate entities: namely, the body and soul. In modern western philosophy, Cartesian dualism has had contradictory outcomes, a result of the problems with Descartes' system. Three modern philosophical currents in the west have opposed Descartes' views: 1. Materialists who reject the spiritual substance of Descartes' philosophy by relying on his opinions on animals (whose life he had considered to be mechanical), who also explain the human being in mechanical terms; 2. Idealists who, relying on the independent spiritual substance posited by Descartes, consider matter to be a form of soul, and deny material substance; 3. Phenomenologists who deny the material and the spiritual substance proposed by Descartes, and posit phenomena that have none of the characteristics of Descartes' substances.

Conclusion:

Both Descartes and Mulla Sadra founded new theories; these theories led to two contradictory conclusions in the history of philosophy. Malebranche, Spinoza, and Leibniz, who are associated with Cartesianism, attempted to solve the contradictions in Descartes' philosophical system, including the question of the nature of the soul. Their efforts resulted in the collapse of the Cartesian system and the appearance of the schools of Materialism, Idealism and Phenomenology in the west. In contrast, Mulla Sadra's philosophical system withstood the criticisms of theologians, and not only did not collapse after his lifetime, but has been enriched and expanded by philosophers such as Mulla Hadi Sabzawari, Mulla Ali Nuri, Mulla Abdullah Zonuzi and Mirza Mehdi Ashtiyani. In the twentieth century, the New Sadrean philosophy appeared. New Sadrean philosophy is a dynamic, current philosophical system, engaged in answering new questions, and forming a new arrangement and organisation of Islamic philosophy. The most distinguished figures in this school are Allamah Muhammad Hussain Tabatabai, Ayatullah Muhammad Baqir Al-Sader, Ayatullah Murtadha Muttahari, Ayatullah Seyyed Muhammad Hussain Beheshi, Imam Mussa Sader, Allamah Muhammad Taqi Ja'fari, Dr. Mehdi Ha'ri Yazdi, Ayatullah Jawadi Amuli, Dr Mehdi Mohaqeq, Ayatullah Seyed Mohammad Khamenei, and Professor Seyyed Hossein Nasr.

Bibliography:

Aristotle. *The Complete works of Aristotle*. Edited by Johnathan Barnes. The Revised Oxford Translation. Princeton, 1995.

Descartes, Rene. *Mediations and other Metaphysical Writings*. London: Penguin, 2003.

Mulla Sadra. *Asfar*. Qum, 1379.

Mulla Sadra. *Shawahed al-Rububiyyah*. Edited by Seyed Jala al-Din Ashtyani. Tehran, 1360.

Mulla Sadra. *Arshiyyah*. Edited by Gholamhussein Ahani. Tehran, 1361.

Thomas, Henry, *The Great Philosophers*, translated by Badrehei, Feraidun, Tehran. 1365.

Endnotes:

1. Aristotle, *De Anime* II, 1. 412 a 27; 4/2 b. line 5
2. Mulla Sadra, *Asfar* (Qum, 1379), vol IV, 1., p 4lines 3ff, p35, last line ff.
3. Ibid., vol IV, 1., p4, lines 3ff, p 35, last line ff.
4. Mulla Sadra, *Arshiyyah* (Tehran, 1361), al-Mashriq al-Thani, Ishraq al-Awwal, Qawa'id 1 and 2.
5. Mulla Sadra, *Shawahid al-Rububiyyah* (Tehran, 1360), third mashhad, third Ishraq.
6. Mulla Sadra, *Arshiyyah*, 50, 238.
7. "The word *form* has been used in a number of ways throughout the history of philosophy and aesthetics. It was early applied to Plato's term *eidos*, by which he identified the permanent reality that makes a thing what it is, in contrast to the particulars that are finite and subject to change. The Platonic concept of form was itself derived from the Pythagorean theory that intelligible structures (which Pythagoras called numbers), and not material elements, gave objects their distinctive characters. Plato developed this theory into the concept of "eternal form," by which he meant the immutable essence that can only be "participated in" by material, or sensible, things. Plato held that eternal forms, though they were not tangible, were of a higher reality than material objects.

For practical purposes, Aristotle was the first to distinguish between matter (*hypokeimenon* or *hyle*) and form (*eidos* or *morphe*). He rejected the abstract Platonic notion of form and argued that every sensible object consists of both matter and form, neither of which can exist without the other. For Aristotle, matter was the undifferentiated primal element; it is that from which things develop rather than a thing in itself. The development of particular things from this germinal matter consists in differentiation, the acquiring of the particular forms of which the knowable universe consists. Matter is the potential factor, form the actualizing factor. (Aristotle further posited the existence of a prime mover, or unmoved mover, i.e., pure form separate from matter, eternal and immutable.)

Thus according to Aristotle, the matter of a thing will consist of those elements of it which, when the thing has come into being, may be said to have become it; and the form is the arrangement or organization of those elements, as the result of which they have become the thing which they have. Thus, bricks and mortar are the matter that, given one form, become a house, or, given another, become a wall. As matter they are potentially anything that they can become; it is the form which determines what they actually become. Here "matter" is a relative term, for a brick on the pile, while potentially part of a house, is already actually a brick; i.e., it is itself a composite of form and matter, clay being matter to the brick as the brick is to the house or to the wall. Matter is that which is potentially a given object but which actually becomes that object only when it is given the right form.

Aristotle's notion of form combines with his teleological viewpoint to give the conclusion that formal development has a direction and may have a goal and that some things are more informed than others. Bricks are more informed than clay, and a house more than bricks.

The Aristotelian concept of form was uniquely adapted to Christianity by Thomas Aquinas, whose works mark the high point of the medieval Scholastic tradition. Aquinas further delineated the concept of form to include "accidental form," a quality of a thing that is not determined by its essence; "sensible form," that element of form that can be distinguished from matter by sense-perception; and other such distinctions. Other Scholastic philosophers, including John Duns Scotus and William of Ockham, worked with the Aristotelian concept of form, but none to as great an effect as Aquinas. For the 18th-century German philosopher Immanuel Kant, form was a property of mind; he held that form is derived from experience, or, in other words, that it is imposed by the individual on the material object. In his *Kritik der reinen Vernunft* (1781, 1787; *Critique of Pure Reason*) Kant identified space and time as the two forms of sensibility, reasoning that, though humans do not experience space and time as such, they cannot experience anything except in space and time. Kant further delimited 12 basic categories that act as structural elements for human understanding." (http://www.britannica.com/EBchecked/topic/213675/form)

8. Mulla Sadra, *Arshiyyah.*, 59-60, 241.
9. Ibid., 61-62, 242.
10. Mulla Sadra, *Asfar*, vol 8, 392.
11. See Descartes, *Principles of philosophy*, principle 60.
12. Ibid., principle 63.
13. See Descartes, *Discourse on the Method*, chapter 5.
14. The greats of philosophy, 179.
15. See Descartes, *Meditations on First Philosophy*.
16. Mulla Sadra, *Asfar*, vol 8, 382.

Index

A

'Abd al-Razzaq Kashani, 75
'Abd al-Razzaq Lahiji, 16
Absolute Being, 87
Absolute Perfect Being, 87
Absolute Truth, 32, 116
"acquired intellect" (*'aql bi al mustafad*), 9, 118
acquired knowledge, 53
active (*fi'li*) intellectual (*'aqli*), 98
"active intellect" (*'aql fa'al*), 84, 88-89, 118-19, 127
actuality, 50, 85-88, 90-92, 95, 110, 125-29
Ajwibah al-masail al-nasiriyyah, 17
'Ala' al-Dawla Simnani, 75
Alexander of Aphrodisias, 61, 89
Al-Hikmah al-'arshiyyah, 17
Al-Hikmat al-muta'aliyah fi'l-asfar al-arba'ah, 18
al-Khafri, 69
All-Hearing, 105, 108-9
All-Seeing, 105, 108-9
Al-Mabda' wa'l Ma'ad, 17
Al-Shawahid al-Rububiyyah, 17, 22, 122
Al-Tasawwur wa'l-tasdiq, 23
Al-'Ulama' al-Zhiriyyun, 76
Anaxagoras, 61
Anselm, 8, 83
Aristotelian, 57, 59, 83-84, 86, 88-89, 107-8, 112
Aristotle, 8, 15, 45-46, 49, 59, 61-63, 67, 83-92, 106-7, 109-10, 112-13, 125, 134-37
Asfar, 7, 14, 19, 29-30, 40, 54, 64-65, 81-82, 93, 96, 98-101, 103, 105-7, 126
Asrar al-Ayat, 17, 19, 24
attribute, 98-101, 104-5
'Awarif al-Ma'rif, 75
'Ayn al-Quzat Hamadani, 74

B

Beautiful Names, 96
Beauty, 99
Being, 55, 59, 87, 109
Bodily Resurrection, 49, 60
brief reason, 8, 117

C

carnal soul, 116
Cartesian Dualism, 130, 134
Causality, 55, 87, 100
Causation, 54, 59, 87, 103
Chain of Causes, 86
contingency, 9, 55, 62, 94-95, 97, 99, 104, 130
contingency of deficiency, 99
contingency of essence, 93-94, 99
cosmological proofs, 8, 83
Creator, 91, 103, 106, 109, 116

D

Dashtaki, 69
Dawwani, 69
deism, 107
demiurge, 8, 83
Descartes, René, 9, 124-25, 130-35
Designer, 8, 83
direct knowledge, 105
Discursive reason, 117
Divine Attributes, 98, 101
Divine Essence, 94, 99, 107, 121
Divine Intellect (*'Aql Rabani*), 116
Divine Unity, 43, 63, 92
Diwan shi'r, 23

E

efficient cause, 57, 88, 91
Empedocles, 61
epistemology, 20
Essence, 14, 18, 39, 41, 46, 93-96, 98-109
essential (*dhati*), 98
Existence, 18, 30, 37-39, 51-53, 55, 93, 95, 104, 106, 131

existence of God, 18, 84, 87, 89, 93-94, 106

F

Faculty of Imagination, 47
faithful intellect (*'Aql-Imani*), 116
Fayz Kashani, 16
final cause, 57, 86, 91
fine light, 116
First Cause, 87
First intellect, 8, 116

G

Ghazali, 48, 60, 67, 70-71
God, 8, 14-15, 18, 26, 30, 33, 60, 63, 72, 75, 83-84, 87, 89-94, 97-103, 105-10, 115-17, 120, 131, 134
God's Oneness, 97
gradated unity, 96
Greek philosophy, 15, 112-13
Greek thought, 91, 109

H

"habitual intellect" (*'aql bi al-malakeh*), 9, 118
Hikmat al-Ishraq, 21, 45, 65-66, 78, 126
honourable intellect (*'Aql Sharif*), 116

I

Ibn al-'Arabi, 74
Ibn Sina, 15, 21, 42-43, 45, 47, 53, 59, 64, 72, 76, 78, 80
Ikhwan al-Safa, 59, 68-69, 77, 81
Iksir al-'arefin, 19
illuminative intellect, 120
illuminative intuition, 105

imaginalia, 88
Immortality, 132
intellect, 8, 12-13, 21, 31-32, 34-37, 43, 47, 50-51, 53-54, 57, 61, 63-64, 66-67, 88-89, 115-21, 123, 127-30, 132
intellect and Revelation, 34
intellect in act (*'aql bi al-fi'l*), 9, 118
Intellection, 34, 51-52, 65-66, 104, 126, 128
"intellect of actuality" ('aql bi al-fi'l), 126-27
"intellect of potentiality" (*'aql bi al-quwwah*), 126
Invalidity of reincarnation, 48
Islam, 11, 27, 70, 84, 88
Islamic Philosophy, 9, 15-16, 18, 30, 54, 61, 65, 135

K

Kasr Asnam al-Jahiliyyah, 17
Khwja 'Abdullah Ansari, 75
Knowledge, 9, 12-14, 19, 30, 33, 36, 39, 42, 44, 46, 51-54, 63, 68, 71-72, 76, 88, 91, 100-101, 104-5, 108-9, 118, 120-21, 127-28, 133
knowledge by presence, 53
"knowledge forms" (*suwar-al-ilmiyyah*), 120
Knowledge of Allah, 43

L

Lambda, 89, 91
Life of God, 91
love, 101, 104-5, 109

M

Mafitih al-Ghaib, 17

Magna Moralia, 92, 113
Majlesi, Mohammad Baqer, 16
"material reason" (*'aql hayuluni*), 8, 117-18
Matnawi, 28
mechanical philosophy, 133
Metaphysics, 77, 86-92, 112-13, 123
method, 26, 31, 43, 53, 65, 93-95, 107, 133, 137
Mir Damad, 11, 15, 24, 26, 37, 41, 59, 67-68, 81
Mirza Mehdi Ashtiyani, 135
monotheism, 20, 44, 84
Mulla Abdullah Zonuzi, 135
Mulla Ali Nuri, 135
Mulla Sadra, 7-9, 11-12, 14-16, 18-22, 24-25, 28-32, 34, 36-38, 40-46, 48-49, 54-56, 58-69, 71-74, 76, 82, 92-93, 95-103, 105-10, 112-13, 115, 117, 120-21, 124-30, 132-37
Mutashabihat al-Quran, 17
mysticism, 65

N

Nasr, Seyyed Hossein, 59, 77-78, 80-81, 135
Necessary Being, 41, 44, 57, 93-98, 100-109
Necessary Existent, 8, 38, 41, 44, 53, 86, 106
Neoplatonic, 88, 113
Ni'matullahi, 16
Nurbakhshi, 16

O

Oneness, 96-97, 100, 107
ontological, 8, 51, 54, 83, 87

P

partial reason, 8, 117
particulars, 32, 98
perception, 18, 51-52, 63, 65, 132
perfect intellect (*'Aql kamil*), 8, 116
Perfection, 9, 17, 36, 45, 53, 56, 58, 62, 71, 88, 95-96, 99, 101-5, 108-10, 116-18, 125, 127-28
physical resurrection, 9, 125
physical senses, 116, 132
Plato, 44-46, 59, 61, 63, 68, 81, 88, 102, 132, 136
Platonic Ideas, 45, 61
popular reason, 8, 117
Porphyry, 59, 61, 63, 102
Possibility of the Nobler, 87
potential intellect / bil-quwah, 118
potentiality, 50, 85, 88, 90, 95, 102, 118, 125-28
Practical intellect, 8-9, 116-19
pre-eternal, 46, 85-87, 91, 102, 105, 107, 109-10
prehension, 51-53
Primary Cause, 56
Primary intelligibles, 54
prime cause, 87
Prime Unmoved Mover, 8, 83
"principality of Being" (*asalat wujud*), 9, 120
principality of existence, 37
the principle of the possibility of the superior, 49
proof for the existence of God, 106
proof of the highly veracious, 93-97, 106
Pythagoras, 18, 61, 136

Q

Qaysari, 32, 78
Qunawi, 60, 74

Qur'an, 7, 18-19, 22-24, 32-36, 50, 72, 74, 98-99, 103, 108, 121, 125

R

ratio, 115
rational soul, 117
Razi, Fakhr al-, 60-61, 66, 72-73
Real (*haqiqi*), 99
Relational (*idafi*), 99
religion, 32, 34-36, 40, 49, 67, 69-71, 75-76, 107
resurrection intellect, 8, 117
Risalah al-huduth, 17
Rumi, 8, 11, 28-29, 75, 116-17, 121-23

S

Sabzawari, 135
sacred Divine Essence, 99
secondary logical intelligibles, 54
secondary philosophical intelligibles, 54
self-consciousness, 91
sensation, 51-53, 91, 104-5, 108
sensibilia, 88
sensory (*hissi*), 98
Shahristani, 61, 67
Shahrzuri, 61
Sharh al-Hidayah, 17, 19
Sharh al-Usul min al-Kafi, 17, 25, 82
Shaykh Ishraq, 45
Sheikh Bahia, 15
Sih Asl, 23, 28, 82
simplicity, 43-44, 46, 95-96, 100-101, 132
Socrates, 61
Soul, 9, 11-14, 18, 22, 28, 33, 35, 42, 46-48, 50-51, 61, 63, 70, 75, 78-79, 113, 118-21, 124-35
speculative intellect, 115, 126
spiritual love, 121

spiritual world, 116-17, 125, 129
substance, 9, 12, 18, 31, 40, 42, 52, 68, 90, 104, 125-26, 128-34
Suhrawardi, 21, 65, 75, 78-79, 81, 93, 102, 105

T

Tafsir Ayah al-Kursi, 17
Tafsir Ayah al-Nur, 17, 29
Tafsir Surah al-'A'la, 17
Tafsir Surah al-Baqarah, 17
Tafsir Surah al-Hadid, 17
Tafsir Surah al-Hamd, 17
Tafsir Surah al-Jumu'ah, 17
Tafsir Surah al-sajdah, 17
Tafsir Surah al-Tariq, 17
Tafsir Surah al-Waqi'ah, 17
Tafsir Surah al-Zilzal, 17
Tafsir Surah Yasin, 17
Ta'liqat al-Shifa', 17
Ta'liqat Hikmah al-Ishrjq, 17
Tankabuni, 16
Tariqah, 16
Temporal Createdness of The Material World, 41
the Ancient Metaphysician, 60
the attributes of perfection, 101
the cosmos, 8, 26, 83, 107
the fundamentality of existence, 37-38, 56, 58-59, 95-96
the glorious intellect, 116
the Gnostics, 38, 73
the graduation of existence, 95
the hierarchy of existence, 9, 120
the hierarchy of the faculties of knowledge, 9, 120
the impossibility of infinite regress, 59, 85, 106
the intelligent, 42, 51, 54, 63
the intelligible, 21, 42, 51, 54, 63, 87

theism, 107
the Literalists, 76
the middle term, 106-7
Theoretical intellect, 8-9, 116, 118, 120
the possible intellect, 89
The Priority of Actuality, 85
the proof of motion, 106
the Seven Leaders, 101
the simplicity of existence, 95
the spiritual traveller, 107
Thinking of the Thought, 91
Thought, 59, 88, 91, 122
Transcendent Philosophy, 7, 30-31, 76, 78-79, 81, 92-93, 98, 108, 122-24
Trans-Substantial Motion, 40
Truth in Its Simplicity Contains All Things, 44
Tusi, 32, 42, 66-67, 105

U

Ultimate Cause of the Universe, 91
Union Of The Intelligent And The Intelligible, 42
unity of existence, 16, 38-39
Universal Intellect, 8, 12, 116
universals, 98
unmoved mover, 8, 90, 92, 106, 110, 136

W

world of intellects, 118, 132
worship, 92
Wujud, 16, 37, 55

Z

Zeno, 61
Zeta, 90
Zubdat al-Hagha'iq, 74

Printed in Great Britain
by Amazon.co.uk, Ltd.,
Marston Gate.